HARLEY-DAVIDSON Legends

Dieter Rebmann | Horst Rösler | Frank Sander

HARLEY-DAVIDSON
Legends

Schiffer Publishing Ltd

4880 Lower Valley Road • Atglen, PA 19310

First published by HEEL Verlag GmbH as Harley-Davidson Legends © 2008

Translated by: David Johnston

Copyright © 2012 by Schiffer Publishing, Ltd.

Library of Congress Control Number: 2012933555

Cover By Bruce Waters
Type set in Univers Condensed/Clarendon LT Std

ISBN: 978-0-7643-4073-4
Printed in China

Schiffer Books are available at special discounts for bulk purchases for sales promotions or premiums. Special editions, including personalized covers, corporate imprints, and excerpts can be created in large quantities for special needs. For more information contact the publisher:

Published by Schiffer Publishing Ltd.
4880 Lower Valley Road
Atglen, PA 19310
Phone: (610) 593-1777; Fax: (610) 593-2002
E-mail: Info@schifferbooks.com

For the largest selection of fine reference books on this and related subjects, please visit our website at **www.schifferbooks.com**
We are always looking for people to write books on new and related subjects.
If you have an idea for a book, please contact us at
proposals@schifferbooks.com

This book may be purchased from the publisher.
Please try your bookstore first.
You may write for a free catalog.

In Europe, Schiffer books are distributed by
Bushwood Books
6 Marksbury Ave.
Kew Gardens
Surrey TW9 4JF England
Phone: 44 (0) 20 8392 8585; Fax: 44 (0) 20 8392 9876
E-mail: info@bushwoodbooks.co.uk
Website: www.bushwoodbooks.co.uk

CONTENTS

INTRODUCTION 7

MODEL 5D (1909) A Legend Is Born 8

MODEL 7D (1911) The First Evolution of the V-Twin 12

MODEL 10F (1914) The Golden Age of the Motorcycle 18

1000 CCM MILITARY (1917) Harley-Davidson Goes to War 22

SPORT TWIN (1919) The Exotic: Harley-Davidson Pushes Through 28

JH (1928) The First "Two Cam" Motor 30

PEASHOOTER (1928) The Eagle Shoots Peas... 34

MODEL V (1930) At Full Speed into the World Economic Crisis 38

SERVI-CAR (1932) Harley's Long Runner on Three Wheels 42

VLD (1933) Art Nouveau Flatheads 46

EL 61 OHV (1936) The First Knucklehead 50

MODEL U "POLICE" (1937) Law and Order on Two Wheels 54

XA 1000 (1942) The Harley Boxer 60

WLA (1942) The Motorcycle That (Almost) Won the War 64

SPORTSTER (1957) Sportiness and Design for Generations... 68

DUO GLIDE (1964) The Company Flagship 72

ELECTRA GLIDE (1965) Igniting the Electric Spark ... 76

XLCH SPORTSTER (1968) Then Came Bronson ... 80

FL EARLY SHOVEL (1969) A Bit of "Easy Rider" 84

XLCR CAFÉ RACER (1977-1978) ... Good Bike, Bad Timing ... 90

FLT TOUR GLIDE (1980) The Shovel as a Recreational Vehicle 94

FXE SUPER GLIDE (1982) American Lifestyle on Two Wheels 98

XR1000 (1983) The Racer for the Street 102

FXRT SPORT GLIDE (1984) Harley-Davidson's Rolling Secret 106

FLTC TOUR GLIDE ULTRA CLASSIC (1989) Pure American Lifestyle 110

FXDWG DYNA WIDE GLIDE (1993) 90 Years and Not Even a Little Quiet 116

FLSTC HERITAGE SOFTAIL (1997) The Harley for Everyone 120

FXSTB NIGHT TRAIN (1998) Black is Beautiful! 124

FLSTF FAT BOY (1998) Fat Salute to the 95th Birthday 128

VRSCA V-ROD (2001) Harley-Davidson and Porsche – Revolution from Milwaukee and Zuffenhausen 132

FLSTS HERITAGE SPRINGER SOFTAIL (2003) 100 Years of Harley-Davidson 136

VRSCR STREET ROD (2006-2007) It Only Danced Two Summers ... 142

XL 1200 N NIGHTSTER (2008) ... One for the Night 146

FXD DYNA SUPER GLIDE (2008) And the Beat Goes On: 105 Years of Harley-Davidson 150

VRSCDX NIGHT ROD (2008) Street Fighter Deluxe! 156

Harley-Davidson's famous "Number 1," built in 1902 and 1903.
Every Harley-Davidson book normally begins with this motorcycle.
Dieter Rebmann photographed the machine immediately after its restoration in 1998.
Afterwards, this treasure could only be seen behind glass or in studio photos.

INTRODUCTION

For more than two decades Dieter Rebmann has been photographing classic Harley-Davidsons all over the world. In addition to Heel's annual Harley-Davidson calendar, his mammoth work "Ride Free Forever," produced in association with Oluf Zierl, who died much too soon, will forever be a milestone in Harley-Davidson literature.

But time has moved on – and in the last decade, Harley-Davidson has pursued a development tempo that can only be described as breathtaking. The VRSC models, new motors, a completely new Sportster series and the birthday parties marking the company's 100th and 105th jubilees have brought many new models and allowed the older machines to enter the annals of Harley-Davidson history. The birthday year 2008 saw all models generally overhauled or redesigned—an almost unbelievable rejuvenation in times of technical and economic change. Time, therefore, for a new stocktaking of the Harley-Davidson history—and a look at the highlights of 105 years of history.

For the new project, cult photographer Dieter Rebmann secured the services of two scene specialists who have probably photographed more custom bikes than Harley-Davidson has offered model variants in 105 years: Frank Sander and "Motographer" Horst Rösler are the official photographers of the AMD European and World Championship of Custom Bike Building and have traveled the world, on location or with their mobile studio equipment. Their articles and photos have appeared in magazines worldwide—and as experts on the scene and Harley-Davidson history, they know which sources are reliable. In addition to my own experience, in writing this book I drew upon almost all the available literature, company brochures, and information from numerous specialists, so that I could offer the reader interesting brief portraits of each machine in its historical context. A compact history of the most important models—and countless highlights—over 105 years can, of course, never be complete.

In a time of security hysteria and perpetual communication, riding a motorcycle is one last bit of personal freedom—a last bit of time in which one can remain undisturbed. As well, a motorcycle is an unbelievably practical means of transportation in cities—and only someone who has travelled one of the world's dream roads on a motorcycle knows the fascinating perspective of the world enjoyed by a biker, compared to driving the same road in a closed metal box. But there is no need to explain this to the readers of this book.

All errors and omissions are ours, and the available records do not always allow for 100% certainty. Anyone who has measured various motorcycles from the same year on a test stand knows what I'm talking about.

A "See you on the road" from Dieter "The Lens" Rebmann, Frank "Thunder" Sander and Horst "Motographer" Rösler — www.dieter-rebmann.de; www.thunder-media-service.de; and www.motographer.de.

MODEL 5D (1909)
A Legend Is Born

V-Twin in the limelight: the belt still drives the rear wheel directly, but the step from bicycle with motor to motorcycle has been made.

After concentrating on the single-cylinder models in the early years, company founders Harley and Davidson eventually became interested in improved performance. Increasing displacement and obtaining greater performance was an option, but this also entailed risks and problems. The competitors at Indian had turned to twin-cylinder technology some time earlier, thus it was a logical decision to follow this path. Already in 1905, Indian had introduced a power plant to the market from which racing engines were derived, and even then success in long-distance races was a decisive factor in the sales success of a motorcycle. One should not forget that,

at that time, motorcycling was not a hobby, rather a bike was a legitimate mode of transportation, which first and foremost had to be reliable and as comfortable as possible.

And so Harley-Davidson began development of the motor that was to become a legend: the 45° V-Twin. The motor that was to change the company's history was born in Harley-Davidson's again expanded workshop in 1909. Of course the motor was not an entirely new design, and, at the time, the engineers had no idea what they had begun. They had been given the task of developing a powerful and reliable motor

for their designs, and they fell back on proven components.

The motor was supposed to expand and consolidate the marque's success, which, as we know, it did for a long time. It made Harley-Davidson the most successful motorcycle manufacturer in the USA and left Indian, Excelsior, and all the others behind. Most of the components selected for the V-Twin had already been extensively tested, so the designers were very confident that their development would be a technical success. The connecting rods and pistons essentially came from the single-cylinder models. A crankshaft was designed on which both connecting rods ran on one lobe, and the V2 was finished. Not quite... A larger crankcase was made and the bearings were reinforced. The carburetor was a Schebler model which, though rather strange-looking by today's standards, had provided good service in the other models. A Bosch magneto ignited the mixture, which was then expelled through the legendary flap exhaust pipe, of course without any sound-deadening effect. The horizontally-ribbed cylinders and cylinder heads with the automatic exhaust valve were also essentially retained. The problem with the so-called "snifter valve" was that it did not work properly in the changed pressure conditions of the enlarged crankcase.

The motor, with just under 50 cubic inches in two cylinders, nevertheless produced approximately 7 hp and allowed the 5D to reach over 40 mph (70 km per hour). Just 27 examples of the model were built. The main reason was problems with the motor, which was difficult to start, ran roughly, and thus did not meet the requirements of the Harley-Davidson philosophy. Further

development was therefore unavoidable. The increased power was also too much for the bike's power train, causing the drive belt, which still had no tensioning mechanism, to slip off.

As was standard at the time, the motorcycle's frame was designed as a rigid frame and fitted with huge 28-

The V-Twin was started by means of a chain to the rear wheel and the belt drive.

Top: Filigree—the belt drive tended to slip, especially when it rained.

Center: The Bosch magneto ignition.

inch tires. Power transmission was by way of a drive belt, which turned a pulley wheel attached to the axle. Only the rear wheel was fitted with a brake, a so-called freewheel brake. There was a suspension system on the front, a movable fork with two springs. If one wants to look at it that way, it was the predecessor of the springer fork. Mounted on the steel tube frame was a two-piece tank that performed two functions. One side of the tank served as an oil tank for the motor and the other side as a conventional fuel tank. Also in the tank was the control for the additional hand-powered oil pump, which was to remain part of the oil delivery system for a long time. And so in 1909—the same year the FBI was founded—despite initial failure a success story was begun that few other motors in the world would equal. Anyone who has driven a Harley motor will understand why this motor has gone down in history.

The great-grandfather of all Harley forks with sprung swing-arm.

Left: Simple in design: motor and cylinder are joined by four bolts. The cylinder angle of 45° is still a trademark of the big twins from Milwaukee.

Below: Between the fork pipes — Harley-Davidson plaque.

The unmistakable sound and the vibrations, which were are accepted as cult and not as annoying, are a delightful experience which is difficult to describe.

Technical Data
MODEL 5D (1909)

Frame:	Single loop steel tube, rigid
Fork:	Swinging fork with two springs
Motor:	Air-cooled single-cylinder, IOE intake over exhaust port valve with snifter valve, belt drive with leather belt, magneto ignition
Cylinders:	1
Displacement:	30.17 cubic inches
Output:	approximately 7 hp
Construction Year:	1909 - 1910

MODEL 7D (1911)
The First Evolution of the V-Twin

Enormous technical advances were achieved in the first decade of general motorization. In the USA, the large-volume V-Twin became the common standard, with marques like Indian, Thor, and Reading-Standard equipping their motorcycles with such motors, not least in order to make their still rather weakly-powered bikes capable of carrying a sidecar. After several years of futile efforts to obtain greater performance from their snifter valve cylinder heads, no way was found around forced control: F-Head, or IOE, the abbreviation for "inlet over exhaust," was the answer for Harley-Davidson. On the Type F motors, the inlet valve sits directly over the exhaust valve, while the spark plug is positioned between the valves at an angle of about 45°. Externally, the F-Head motors are distinguishable by their tappet rods, which are of different lengths: While the exhaust valve is pushed open from directly below, the intake valve is opened by means of a rocker arm. The single-piece cylinders benefited from advances in casting technology: The upper part of the cylinder head has vertical cooling ribs, while horizontal ribs provide an outlet for cooling air flow.

Ignition is provided by a Bosch magneto located behind the motor and powered by a gearwheel cascade. Ignition timing is set by means of a lever system. With a bore of 3 inches

The 7D by Harley-Davidson was the first V-Twin which was up to the technological standards of the day.

and a stroke of 3½ inches, the 800-cc motor produced 6.5 hp, which enabled the machine to reach close to 62 miles per hour (100 kilometers per hour) with a single rider. And this was on a system of roads clearly more suited to ox carts and horse-drawn carriages than modern motor vehicles: On country roads in the USA, asphalt was still a foreign word in those days. And so, on the existing roads, the great advantage of the large-volume V-Twin came to light: the torque from the lowest speed range, which even then pulled the motorcycle from the mud tractor style.

Despite the bulky V-Twin, the Model 7D is still reminiscent of the earliest motorcycles: large spoked wheels and a narrow-profile single tube frame

and, not to be forgotten, the bicycle seat. The belt drive powered the rear wheel directly and with no gearing, and the motor was started with bicycle pedals with a separate belt drive. At least Harley-Davidson provided a belt tensioner that model year, which could also be used as a clutch when the motor was running. Thus, for the first time, Harley did away with the almost impossible balancing act of lifting the bike from the main stand and folding it with the motor running and the motorcycle trying to roll away without a rider. In several rest positions belt slippage could even be controlled to a certain extent: convenient when it was raining or the engine oiling. To say nothing of city traffic with constant stop and go, for one must not forget: The motorcycle still shared the streets almost exclusively with horse-drawn carriages and streetcars. Automobiles were still a rarity.

The redesigned tank integrated gasoline and oil reservoirs, and the motor was lubricated by loss lubrication. The price of oil and environmental protection were not considerations in those days. The large tool kit was no decoration: Flat tires on the bad roads were a bother for drivers—and many lubrication nipples on the motor, drive train, and linkages craved slippery fluid. The

[13]

tool kit enabled the driver to virtually disassemble and repair the motorcycle, but if metal parts needed mending, he was forced to turn to the nearest blacksmith.

The year 1911 was important in the history of the Harley-Davidson company, for with the ongoing boom in motorization management decided on another expansion on Juneau Avenue: A bank loan from Marshall & Isley provided the cornerstone for an important expansion in production. In 1911, Harley-Davidson had 481 employees, but in the following year this figure rose to 1,076. The number of motorcycles built, however, dropped from 5,625 in 1911 to 3,852 in 1912, probably because of the expansion, for by 1913, Harley-Davidson was producing more than 13,000 motorcycles a year. The motorcycle boom in the USA was on its way to its true high point—and Harley-Davidson was firmly determined to secure its slice of the pie. Harley-Davidson successfully went after customers with an aggressive advertising campaign: "The most comfortable, most economic and easiest to start machine on the market!" boasted the advertisements. The ads were aimed mainly at business people, who would use the motorcycles to deliver their wares.

Left: Still with spokes— rear wheel 1911.

Right: Perfectly restored—front fork and steering head.

Left: A gem for any motorcycle rider in 1911— Harley-Davidson 7D.

Below Left: Before the First World War, the bicycle seat was the standard.

Technical Data
MODEL 7D (1911)

Frame:	Single loop steel tube, rigid
Fork:	Springer
Motor:	Air-cooled V2, IOE intake over exhaust port valve, belt drive with leather belt, magneto ignition
Cylinders:	2, 45° cylinder angle
Displacement:	50 cubic inches
Output:	approximately 7 hp
Construction Year:	1911

MODEL 10F (1914)
The Golden Age of the Motorcycle

Anyone who, on 1 January 1914, would have claimed that by the end of the year there would be a line of trenches extending from the Belgian Channel Coast to the Swiss border, would probably have been called crazy—especially in the USA. While in Europe, timid efforts were being made to motorize the armed forces, with motorcycles envisaged as mobile machine-gun carriers. The American army was in the same state it had been during the last Indian wars: The cavalry rode against the Mexican bandits of Pancho Villa on the same horses as they had against Sitting Bull and Crazy Horse. Not until 1916 was the viability of motorized vehicles tested in an expedition against Villa. By then

the warring parties in Europe had gone farther: The shots in Sarajevo in June 1914 were the initial spark that would lead, in August, to a world conflict that would forever change the world, including America.

In the tenth year of its existence, the Harley-Davidson Motor Company was enjoying a steadily expanding customer base. It was the golden age of motorcycles in the USA, for not even the Ford Model T could match the numbers being spat out by the major American motorcycle manufacturers: 60,000 to 70,000 units were built and delivered that year. In 1914, Indian was the largest manufacturer of motorcycles in

Patina from more than 90 years: Harley-Davidson 1914. While, in Europe, the First World War was raging, in America, the motorcycle was enjoying its "golden age."

IOE control—simple
to operate and reliable
in everyday use.
The Bosch magneto
was driven by a
gearwheel cascade.

the world. At $285 dollars, the Model 10F was the top model in the Harley-Davidson product line and 7,956 of this model were built in 1914. While one might chuckle today over $285, one must view the price in the context of the time: In 1914, an industrial worker was paid an average of $2.50 per ten-hour day. It was in 1914 that Henry Ford caused a sensation by doubling this starvation wage—in part because this pay increase would enable his workers to purchase the automobiles they were assembling. The equivalent value of a Harley-Davidson 10F was 57 working days.

From a technical standpoint the F-Head motor had changed little since its introduction in 1911—the progress lay in the equipment and the details: displacement had risen to 61 cubic inches (988 cc), the drive train was covered by a metal shield and the two-speed hub gearshift better exploited the available motor performance. The clutch and brakes were pedal operated, an arrangement that soon had to prove its effectiveness in city traffic: the first street light was set up at an intersection in Cleveland, Ohio, home to several makers of motorcycles.

Other parts of the motorcycle were now made by Harley-Davidson itself instead of being purchased. These included the hubs and the newly-developed drum brakes, which applied

Grease nipple on
the front fork and a
simple odometer.

Right: Wide and comfortable – the saddle from 1914.

braking pressure by means of internal brake shoes. Braking effectiveness was significantly better—which in view of the traffic in the large cities was of vital importance.

Even if the original Renault Gray has given way to rust brown, the hand-painted decorative stripes are still visible—and the discussion begins: original condition or restoration? What to one observer is just a useless pile of rust with no value, is to the enthusiast the epitome of authenticity. Original paint and decorative stripes are very popular, no matter how much rust is present. As time passes, it becomes ever more difficult to find Harley-Davidsons that are really authentic and in original condition. The "shed discoveries" of the 70s and 80s have been more or less exhausted and it is more important to preserve those motorcycles in original condition and not "restore them to death."

Anyone who can call a 10F in this condition of noble patina of a century of motorcycle history his own, does not need to worry about rust. And with accessories, the machine can be even more valuable! If the part still works in this condition, then all the better! In

general, the rule applies that the more contemporary original parts there are on a classic, the more desirable it is to preserve it in its existing condition. The machine can always be restored, but original condition comes only once.

Left: Horn and light.

Right: Additional light, normally used on police machines.

Only the tires are new – even a little patina doesn't hurt, as long as the machine is drivable.

Below Left: Original paint from 1914 and the simple two-speed gearshift on the rear hub.

Technical Data
MODEL 10F (1914)

Frame:	Single loop steel tube, rigid
Fork:	Springer
Motor:	Air-cooled V2, IOE intake over exhaust port valve, chain drive, magneto ignition
Cylinders:	2, 45° cylinder angle
Displacement:	60.34 cubic inches
Output:	approximately 10 hp
Construction Year:	1911

1000 CCM MILITARY (1917)
Harley-Davidson goes to War

In 1917, the First World War was in full swing and the German fleet was attacking American ships with growing frequency. After the presidential election in the USA, the reelected President Wilson received authority from the congress to join the war. As Harley-Davidson had become involved in the development of military machines, America's entry into the war resulted in a tremendous upswing for the company. To a large extent, William Harley personally introduced motorcycles and the new developments to the military. This gave him the advantage of learning about any requests or modifications first hand. This groundwork also resulted in an immediate increase in production.

Although the war would only last another year, in that period, approximately 20,000 motorcycles were sent to Europe for military purposes, of which about one third were made by Harley-Davidson. It was intended that the motorcycles should be used as reconnaissance and courier vehicles by the American troops and of course the bikes received modifications such as weapons mounts, etc. According to unconfirmed reports and photos, it was a 1917 model driven by a certain Roy Holtz that became the first American vehicle to cross the German border on 11 November 1918.

Harley-Davidson's first warhorse: olive green was the standard finish.

During the war, the British suspended production of civilian motorcycles, which resulted in a growing interest in the American V-Twins that spread over all of Europe. Harley-Davidson's clever marketing strategy, not to convert all of its manufacturing capacity to military vehicles, instead adding personnel to make even more machines, paid off. Approximately fifty percent of the motorcycles produced were civilian machines, which, thanks to reports of their reliability, found a growing level of acceptance. Harley changed the classic gray color to olive green for that production year, and development was pushed ahead with full force. Despite the rising cost of raw materials, the Americans were forced to produce their own bearings, wheels, and magnetos,

as the war made deliveries of many parts from overseas no longer possible. German-made Bosch ignitions could no longer be obtained, so as the production year went on, the ignition system was changed to an American product. The problem was, especially on the military machines, that a problem with the ignition often meant replacement of the entire system. With the improving quality and higher performance of the V-Twins, sales of the Single models fell off sharply. More V-Twins were built, and they were also more technically complex. For this reason, in 1917, Harley-Davidson founded the Service School in Milwaukee. There members of the military, but also dealers from the now almost worldwide network of dealers, were trained. The Model J with a displacement of 61 cubic inches

Rust patina: the cast iron cylinders were susceptible to rust.

Right: Horn and headlight, the latter with a slotted cover to prevent being seen by the enemy. For most of the war the Germans held the higher ground and any movement by vehicles immediately drew artillery fire.

(988 cc) and the classic V-Twin was by then available with a variety of options, including a sidecar, various types of tires, etc.

Already in 1917, the J model had 16-17 hp, capable of propelling the motorcycle to a maximum speed of about 65 miles per hour (105 kilometers per hour). It had a three-speed gearbox and a chain drive with tensioning mechanism, which could be adjusted manually.

Braking was by means of a band brake on the rear wheel, which was activated by a rod with bell crank. There was no front brake on bikes from this model year. A characteristic of this

model was the prominent tank-mounted speedometer, which was driven by means of a shaft and a sprocket on the drive chain. Also prominent were the indentations on the right half of the tank, which were needed to provide sufficient room for the valve train tappets. Weighing 324.4 pounds (147 kilograms), by modern standards it was a true lightweight, which was to pay off in military service and the countless races in which the J took part. While there was no rear suspension, up front there was an improved suspension fork, which was intended to improve comfort. The seat was cushioned by a self-contained spring system, which

Lockable: the rear brake could be locked—especially for use with a sidecar.

Assembled: military motorcycles were delivered as a "bike in the box." The wheels and handlebars were installed by the troops.

Below: US Army inventory number on the tank.

improved rider comfort on the still very uneven roads of the day. Approximately 9,100 examples of the Model J were built in 1917, with the civilian version costing $310.

Technical Data
1000 CCM MILITARY (1917)

Frame:	Single loop steel tube, rigid
Fork:	Swinging fork with two springs
Motor:	Air-cooled V2, IOE intake over exhaust port valve, belt drive with leather belt, battery coil ignition
Cylinders:	2, 45° cylinder angle
Displacement:	60.30 cubic inches
Output:	approximately 16-17 hp
Construction Year:	1917-1918

SPORT TWIN (1919)
The Exotic: Harley-Davidson Pushes Through

Professionally restored: The Sport Twin was the first postwar Harley, aimed especially at a customer group of motorsport enthusiasts.

Harley-Davidson and racing—for many unimaginable. But at the beginning of the Twentieth Century, it was Harley-Davidson that was breaking almost all of the records. Whether on oval courses, long or short road races, or endurance races, Harley was almost unbeatable.

Some of the racing machines were street bikes that had been modified by their owners, but most of the successes were achieved by sport models specially developed by the company. One of these bikes was the 1919 Sport Twin, which unlike the more familiar models, had a flat twin engine installed longitudinally. In 1919, it became apparent that Harley's decision to continue making civilian machines during the war had

been correct. The popularity of the V-Twins grew steadily, and so putting this motorcycle with a boxer motor on the market was a gamble. In the USA, the bike was only very popular with race drivers; however, in England and Europe sales were considerably better. The year the Sport Twin appeared on the market, Bill Ottaway, R.W. Enos, and C.C. Wilborn reorganized Harley-Davidson's legendary Wrecking Crew. The race team consisted of experienced prewar riders and young talents who were trained by Harley and provided with the best possible equipment. Long-distance races and regularity races continued to be extremely popular.

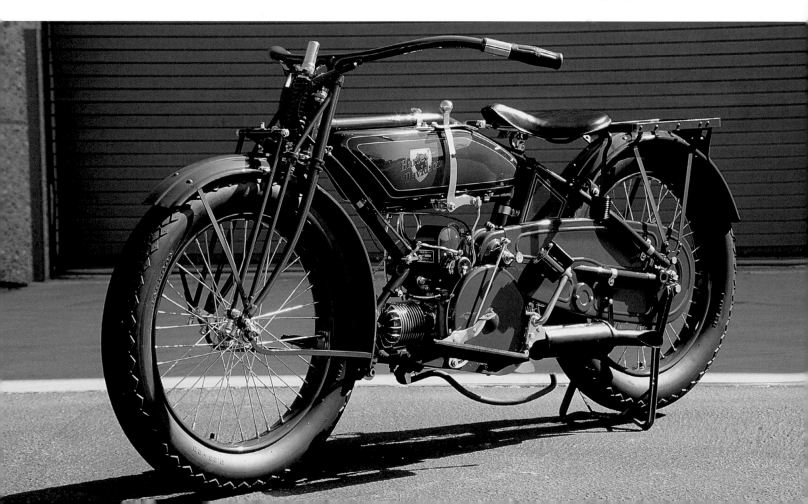

The Americans realized early on, however, that an oval course like those now used for NASCAR races was ideal for the spectator, as it enabled him see most of the course. As well as dirt track races, there were also so-called flat track races, which demanded the utmost of drivers and machines. The races were held in Thunder Domes, also known as death tracks. The wood-planked oval courses with banked curves attracted throngs of spectators and turned the daredevil riders into heroes. Unfortunately, there were many serious accidents, some fatal, and the sport was ended at the end of the 1920s.

With a displacement of just 584 cc, the W Sport Twin's motor produced only about 6 hp; however, the bike weighed just 264 pounds (120 kilograms), making it the terror of the competition. Another advantage was its low center of gravity, a result of the flat twin design. The production version of the Sport Twin had a top speed of about 50 miles per hour (80 kilometers per hour) and it arrived on the market as an extremely reliable and easy to maintain motorcycle. One technical peculiarity was the sealed chain box, which reduced chain wear during long-distance races. The carburetor was specially protected against dust and even the fuel lines were relocated to the handlebars.

The motor possessed several special features that would not be used by other makers until much later. For example, all valves were operated by a camshaft, which considerably reduced the moving masses in the motor. Of course, as a result, the motor achieved high revolutions more easily, which was a considerable advantage in racing. The motorcycle was equipped with a three-speed gearbox which was operated by means of a foot clutch and hand shifter. The steel tube frame had no rear suspension but at the front there was an open spring shock absorber. The sprung seat formed a single unit with the tank and baggage carrier, giving the motorcycle a very sporty appearance.

Until production ended in 1923, the Sport Twin was equipped with rear brakes only. The motorcycle ran on 26-inch rims, on which were mounted 3 x 26 tires. In 1919, the

Above: Because of its design, the horizontally-opposed motor was almost vibration-free. Note the large flywheel on the left side of the motor and the magneto above.

Left: Carburetor on the rear cylinder.

The right side of the motor was dominated by the encapsulated flywheel and the high-mounted—and likewise enclosed—chain case. Clearly visible are the foot clutch and kick starter.

motor was only available with magneto ignition. Beginning in 1920, however, an ignition system with electrical lighting could also be obtained. Of the 9,073 Sport Twins that were built, just 2,569 had the electrical system, which suggests that the majority of the motorcycles sold were purchased as sport bikes.

With a price of $335, the Sport Twin was a sports machine for the ambitious amateur, which was still affordable and very competitive, as its many victories prove.

The motorcycle was also very easy to maintain and all components were readily accessible, a decisive advantage in long-distance races. Harley-Davidson

Carburetor inlet channel with long inlet manifold with sharp curves and exhaust collector were combined in a single component. In 1919, the designers were obviously still unaware of the relationship between inlet air temperature and engine performance.

Sporting line: one of the most extraordinary Harley-Davidson models in the marque's history and also a path that could have been taken successfully. Today, a sought-after collectors' model.

rider Hap Scherer won the New York to Chicago long-distance race, a distance of 1,012 miles, in a record time of 31 hours and 24 minutes. Other big wins by Harley-Davidson riders included two victories in the 200-mile Los Angeles race. Harley riders also took second and third places. This dominance extended throughout the entire country and earned Harley the reputation of being a fast and very reliable motorcycle. The factory team, the so-called Wrecking Crew, of course played a large role in this, and even after their official association ended, it still received support from Harley-Davidson.

Technical Data
SPORT TWIN (1919)

Frame:	Single loop steel tube, rigid
Fork:	Curved swing arm, one shock strut
Motor:	Air-cooled 2-cylinder horizontally-opposed mounted longitudinally in the frame, OHV, magneto ignition, 3-speed transmission, hand operated
Cylinders:	2, 180° cylinder angle
Displacement:	35.64 cubic inches
Output:	approximately 6 hp
Construction Year:	1919-1923

JH (1928)
The First "Two Cam" Motor

At the end of the 1920s, after a quarter century of development, Harley-Davidson gave the seemingly exhausted F-Head models a noisy farewell: The JH Model of 1928 brought the era's racing technology to the road and placed it in the hands of private customers seeking success on the racetrack. On the racetrack and in hill climbing, the twin cam factory machines, some already with OHV valve control and four valves per cylinder, had made customers' mouths water and relegated the competition from Indian to second place. The riders of production models could only dream about the dusty country roads of the far west. In terms of performance, the production motorcycles lagged far behind, causing potential buyers to turn to the Indian Scout 101 or Excelsior's Super X. The complaints reached the ears of the management in Milwaukee. The new side-valve motors were already being tested, but their performance was not yet satisfactory. They, therefore, installed the proven version of the twin cam motor with two displacement variants into the modified chassis of the J and JD models, and the racing machine was ready for the street. Many purchasers of the Two Cam still had memories of Joe Petrali's victories in the back of their heads. In 1925, he had won no less then three board track races with an average speed of over

Whether Two Cam or Twin Cam, the JH's sporting qualities were not recognized. Broad fenders kept the dirt of country roads off the rider.

One may imagine the two camshafts. A set of gears drove the oil pump and ignition magneto.

100 miles per hour (164 kilometers per hour). The prospect of a motorcycle capable of reaching the magic figure of 100 miles per hour inspired many customers to open their wallets, even if the production roadster could only reach about 87 miles per hour (140 kilometers per hour). A strain was already being placed on wallets by the activities of private racers, even those not involved in motorsports: To achieve precise and more direct valve control, the rollers normally found on the tappets were deleted. They took this risk because of the newly-introduced oil pump controlled by the throttle switch. As the oil gauge also had to be done away with, the oil level and oil pump setting had to be carefully checked. The more precise valve control resulted in improved combustion and a noticeable increase in performance. Wear on the chain-driven camshafts was ignored by

riders: depending on the race, privately procured or new camshafts were installed anyway.

The two motor variants differed in bore and stroke: the 61-cubic-inch motor of the JH had a bore-stroke ratio of $3^{5}/_{16}$ to $3\frac{1}{2}$ inches, while the larger 74.66-cubic-inch JDH had a square bore-stroke ratio of $3^{7}/_{16}$ to 4 inches. This made it possible to use the same crankshaft housing for both motorcycles—a huge saving in a time of rising cost pressures. And to underscore the sporting image, both models were given magnesium pistons with an alloy developed by Dow Chemicals nine years earlier. For the racetrack, a limited series of Ricardo F-Head cylinders was produced and sold to selected racers. The compression ration of 1:10 was extraordinary for the time.

Left: The shifter on the left tank half.

Right: Innovation in 1928—front wheel drum brake now on a Harley-Davidson.

That year Harley showed itself to be boldly experimental: Two V4 Flathead motors of 1300 and 1,475 cubic centimeters) were tested, in an effort to match the four-cylinder racing motors of Indian and Excelsior-Henderson. Had they known about their competitors' production costs, they might have taken a different path. In any case the world economic crisis out an end to the experiments—the prototypes disappeared.

Visually, the JH and JDH differed little from their "tame" contemporaries: fenders, springer fork with tool kit, fuel-oil tank with typical cutouts for control of the inlet valves, foot boards, and wide handlebars. What modern-day layman could tell the difference between an Evolution motor and the Twin Cam? The difference could only be seen on the road, if one looked the Two Cam in the exhaust …

One simple detail finally made the Harley-Davidsons from the 1928 model year true "modern" motorcycles, even though its introduction was contentious: the front wheel brake. The 1928 model year was the first to see a sealed drum brake installed in the spoked front wheel. While today it is known that the front brake does two-thirds of the braking work, the riders of the 1920s feared a jammed front wheel and a resulting crash. Given the predominance of gravel and dirt roads, this fear was not entirely unjustified. Some riders went so far as to disconnect the brake cables, fearing a crash more than landing in hedge because of insufficient braking power. Under present road and racetrack conditions, jamming a front wheel is difficult to accomplish. The image of the Two Cam of 1928-29 is entirely comparable with that of the Brough Superior SS 100, later the Vincent Black Shadow, a Münch-4 or even fine modern-day racers modified for the street like the Honda NR 750. The era of the F-Heads ended with a bang—one that followed the crash of the New York stock exchange …

Battery and manufacturer's plate: The latter's engraved numbers show the motorcycle's construction year (28) and type (JH).

Rustic—all the strands came together in the switchbox.

Below: Lamp, horn, and tool box formed part of the standard equipment.

Technical Data
JH (1928)

Frame:	Single loop steel tube, rigid
Fork:	Springer
Motor:	Air-cooled V2, IOE intake over exhaust port valve, 2 camshafts, chain drive, magneto ignition, 3-speed manual transmission
Cylinders:	2, 45° cylinder angle
Displacement:	60.34 cubic inches
Output:	approximately 29 hp
Construction Year:	1928-29

PEASHOOTER (1928)
The Eagle Shoots Peas...

Motorsport in the USA already had a character all its own: With the beginning of motorization at the start of the Twentieth Century, the motorcycle initially conquered the existing road-racing arenas. When speeds increased and races became more dangerous, motorcycles got their own racetracks, often completely made of wood, the "board tracks." The atmosphere of the board tracks, some of them stadia with a mile of track length, must have been breathtaking, for the motorcycles had neither exhaust systems nor brakes and reached speeds of about 100 miles per hour (160 kilometers per hour) and more. After several serious accidents—unlike the Circus Maximus in Rome, racers occasionally jumped the barricades into the crowds—attendance dropped. The United States' entry into the First World War also contributed to their decline. By the end of the war, the wooden tracks had fallen into disrepair and their restoration was not economically feasible. Only a few big stadia survived the 1920s. A suitable replacement was needed and it was found in the many horse racetracks that existed in the USA: The Roaring Twenties saw the birth of the dirt track.

Harley-Davidson had initially left racing to private riders but still boasted about their success: "We can't help

A dominant racehorse from the engine smiths in Milwaukee: the Peashooter with dirt track tires and race ready.

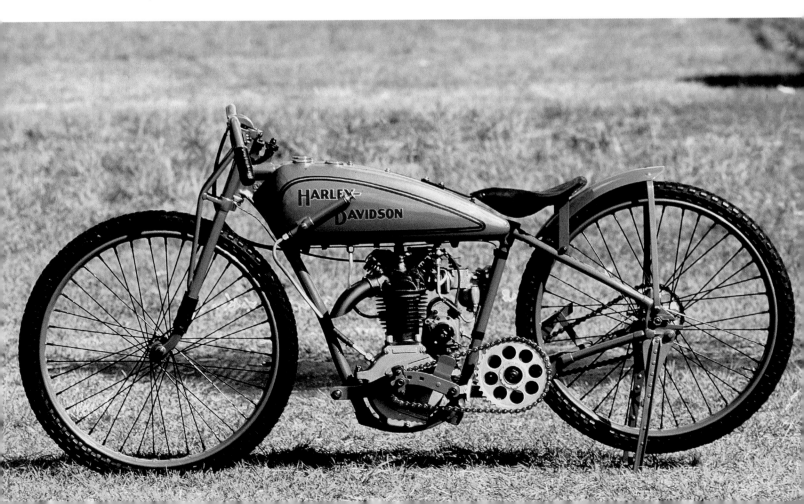

it if other people win races with our machines" went the slogan, but in 1915 the company became fully involved in motorsport.

Involvement in racing soon paid off for Harley-Davidson. The marque's image was characterized by the fast and reliable single- and twin-cylinder machines until well into the war, and when the big manufacturers began dying out after the First World War, victories on the track became a vital advertising tool for the big three of Indian, Harley-Davidson, and Excelsior-Henderson. The new single-cylinder motor was unveiled in 1926: the A, AA, B, and BA models were completely new and could be bought with side-valve and OHV motors. The 21 cubic-inch side-valve model put out a solid 8 hp, while the "hot" OHV singles produced 12 hp—and the factory team still had a few extra horsepower in their tool kits. One of the best known Peashooter riders was Harley legend Joe Petrali. The year before the peashooter was introduced Petrali had won the National Championship and several legendary board track races like the 300-mile (!) race and the 100-mile race in Altoona with an average speed in excess of 100 miles per hour. He finished the 10-mile race in Laurel, Maryland with a speed of 111.18 miles per hour. Petrali cleaned up with the Peashooter and in 1935 won all 13 races in the American Dirt Track Championship. His mount was the Model AA, an excellently restored 1928 model, a pure racing motorcycle for use on the rough dirt tracks in the "wild west" of the USA. The single-cylinder motor was housed in a tubular chassis with rigid rear end—a configuration still used by European Speedway machines and optimal for high-speed cornering. The front fork had minimal spring travel but was fitted

with bracing struts above the springs. In any case, this machine simply drifted through curves. The downward-cranked handlebars enabled the rider to make himself as small as possible on the straight. Only then did the left foot find its way to the forward foot rest. Also on the straight, the rider had time to operate the oil pump on the left side of the tank, while his right hand held the throttle full open. Depending on racing trim, this light motorcycle 239.8 pounds (109 kilograms) could reach speeds in excess of 62 miles per hour (100 kilometers per hour). The final gearing was set according to the track length, for the Peashooter had neither a transmission nor brakes. Consequently, the phrase "he who brakes loses" could not have been coined at that time. Even in the 1920s motorcycle racing was not for the fainthearted. In 1928, the AA was the most produced sport model of the single-cylinder series. Sixty-

Two camshafts, hanging valves, short intake manifold—for 1928 the design of this single-cylinder motor was extremely modern.

A compact assembly— ignition magneto and carburetor.

Below left: Minimal— handlebar clamp and fork bridge.

Below right: The rider had to operate the oil pump by hand.

five examples were built and sold to private riders. Equipment was minimal. Everything on this motorcycle was geared for racing: small rear fender, fixed sports seat, hollow-chain pinions. Few weight-saving options remained, but some owners took the drill to the fender and mounts. Many riders of

the "domesticated" Model B side-valve machines probably dreamed of riding a fast AA; however, 3,482 examples of the B rolled off the Juneau Avenue production line…

The downward-cranked handlebars gave the rider the racing position.

Below: Spartan—racing seat.

Technical Data

A, BA PEASHOOTER (1928)

Frame:	Single loop steel tube, rigid
Fork:	Springer
Motor:	Air-cooled single cylinder, side valve control, chain drive, magneto ignition, 3-speed manual transmission
Cylinders:	2, 45° cylinder angle
Displacement:	21.09 cubic inches
Output:	approximately 8 hp
Construction Year:	1926-28

MODEL V (1930)
At Full Speed Into the World Economic Crisis

The Model V—a machine that Harley-Davidson dealers of the 1930s surely remember with mixed feelings. Not without flaws, this example still has the original paint and accessories.

On 25 October 1929, Groucho Marx's stockbroker called and told his client: "The jig is up. The party's over!" Like many other Americans, the comedian had put much of his wealth into the constantly rising stocks, and within a few days, the entire shaky structure came crashing down. "Black Friday" on the New York Stock Exchange was followed by mass unemployment (an estimated 13 to 15 million workers), widespread business closures, and no less than 5,000 bank failures. Suddenly, a used Model-T Ford could be had for $15 to $75, while luxury automobiles like Cadillac, Pierce-Arrow or Packard could be bought for $100 to $300. Who was

going to put $340 down on the table for a Harley-Davidson "V"—even one that was almost new?

The F-Head power plant, which had been in production since 1911, had reached the limits of its performance after it was fitted with twin cams, and Harley-Davidson subsequently switched entirely to the side-valve motor. Flathead motors made by Ford and other automobile manufacturers had proved their reliability—and the Indian Scout sometimes defeated Harley's OHC racers on the track. Lower production costs were another argument, as was operating reliability. If the inlet valve of an IOE motor (inlet over exhaust) failed,

Original or upgraded?
If the old hardware is
still turning inside the
motor, then the V is
worth a fortune.

it fell into the combustion chamber and destroyed the piston and cylinder. With a side-valve motor this danger was reduced. The 30-V series was also developed with the classic displacement of 74 cubic inches and four versions were delivered in 1930: the V, VL, VS, and VC. The V had a relatively low compression ration of 4:1 and produced just 28 hp at the rear wheel. Only the VS, which was designed for use with a sidecar, had even lower compression (3.6:1); consequently, the power output for two-man operation with a sidecar was catastrophic.

It was bad enough that the V-Class was more than 110 pounds (50 kilograms) heavier than the previous year's J Models, but an engine design error was about to ruin the reputation of Harley-Davidson. From today's point of view, the radical step from the F-Head motors to the Flatheads is difficult to understand. With its production capacity, Harley-Davidson could easily have produced several model lines side by side, and the J models were extremely popular with dealers and the public. Even today,

it is difficult to obtain information from the "Factory" as to who was responsible and the problems that resulted. It is rumored, however, that for marketing reasons the Model D, the 45-cubic-inch Flathead introduced in 1929, and the Model V were sent to the market, without factory trials, one year too soon. The results were fatal: To improve the motor's responsiveness and acceleration, the camshaft had been lightened to the limits of what was practical. The V accelerated quickly, its engine revving furiously, but only to 50 miles per hour, where output suddenly dropped off and vibration became unbearable. No sooner had the first machines been received, assembled, and tested by the dealers, than the complaints began pouring in. Factory trials would surely have revealed these defects, but production had already begun and the machines were being delivered all over the world.

The dealers were in the front line: Disappointed customers demanded their money back and Harley asked for their loyalty.

Left: Tachometer drive
from the rear wheel.

Right: The carburetor.

The development department worked day and night on the problem—and, in weeks, developed a new motor. It had a heavier crankshaft which, because of its increased diameter, required a new motor casing. The new motor casing, of course, required a modified chassis, which was also produced in record time. Harley-Davidson immediately incorporated the changes into production, but the dealers were left to deal with work on the machines already delivered. While they were sent the new parts "on the house," the complete disassembly of the chassis and motor was very time consuming and was done at the cost of the dealership. From the forks to the rear fender, all of the parts had to be removed from the chassis and the motor, disassembled, and then reassembled again. And all this was done without being able to charge one additional cent. More than 1,300 machines are believed to have been affected worldwide. Together with the introduction of the D, this was one of the greatest financial disasters in the history of Harley-Davidson. Some dealers switched to other brands or simply threw in the towel in the face of the economic crisis.

While export sales remained strong at the start of the depression, as the economic crisis spread worldwide there was also a noticeable drop in sales in other countries. In the summer of 1929, the last of the big board tracks was torn down in Rockingham, New Hampshire. That spring the fast racing machines had thundered over the planks one last time—truly, the party was over …

Left: The tachometer
is mounted on
the tank.

Right: The twin
headlights were
only offered for a
short time.

The Model V was also not a huge success in terms of design. This example, still in its original finish, would confirm this even without the rust patina.

Below: The passenger seat—hand grip for the lady.

Technical Data
MODEL V (1930)

Frame:	Single loop steel tube, rigid
Fork:	Springer
Motor:	Air-cooled V2, side valve control, chain drive, battery coil ignition, 3-speed manual transmission
Cylinders:	2, 45° cylinder angle
Displacement:	74 cubic inches
Output:	approximately 30 hp
Construction Year:	1930-1936 V/VL

SERVICAR (1932)
Harley's Long Runner on Three Wheels

As to the question of which model of Harley-Davidson had been in production longest, until a few years ago, the answer was surprising: the Servi-Car! Not until the Sportster series turned fifty in 2007 did it exceed the production life of this robust three-wheeler. Introduced in 1932 and produced until 1973, the ServiCar was Harley's answer to the Indian Despatch Tow, which Harley's great rival had introduced shortly before. Three-wheeled motorcycle conversions for commercial purposes were most common in the Far East, whereas in the USA small shops had gotten by largely with converted sidecar machines with box bodies. The year 1932 was one of the worst of the depression, as the stock market crash of 1929 had depressed economies worldwide. Both manufacturers desperately sought new markets and new product ideas. It was not exactly helpful that, in the British Commonwealth, the import duty on American goods was thirty percent, while that for English goods had fallen to zero. Harley could not compete with this price advantage. High unemployment meant that private individuals in the USA were finding it difficult to free up the funds needed to purchase new motorcycles, leaving the police and commercial enterprises

New customers urgently sought: First produced in 1932, the ServiCar was a versatile machine and was built until the 1970s.

45-cubic-inch forever: Thanks to the Servi-Car the side-valve motors were built until the 1970s.

as the sole remaining markets. The Servi-Car derived its name from its function: the automobile service industry. Even then, garages capitalized on customer service: Mechanics picked up automobiles from the customers and after inspection or servicing also returned them. To avoid having to send along a second man, the ServiCar had a tow hook on the front fork. The three-wheeler was attached to the car's bumper and towed back to the garage. When the work was done, the mechanic returned the car to the customer and then drove the three-wheeler back to the garage. The large box offered sufficient room for tools and spare parts for breakdown service—but with a little over 28 hp, the machine lacked the power needed to tow the huge luxury automobiles of the 1930s, which often weighed between one and two tons.

Another function was aimed at traffic control. For this reason, the throttle control was moved to the left side of the handlebars and a special low-geared gearbox for slow speeds was installed. Standard equipment also included a chalk stick, with which the ServiCar's rider could comfortably mark the tires of parked vehicles. When the parking time was up, a ticket was guaranteed. ServiCars were used by local traffic police and were a familiar sight in American cities until the 1970s. Even the Meter Maids rode comfortably on their police trikes, issuing their quota of parking tickets. This Harley model was probably cursed more by automobile drivers than any other motorcycle in history.

The first ServiCar of 1932 had a 45-cubic-inch Model D flathead—with reduced compression for low speeds. A support frame supported the transport box and the rear axle. Four different models were offered, the G, GA, GE, and GD. The rear wheels were chain-driven, and the axle, derived from an automobile design, had a differential. The sturdy luggage box was made of pressed metal sheet, and the first models still had spoked wheels, which were soon replaced by the typical disc wheels. A parking brake made it possible to park the three-wheeler even on a slope. In the 1933 model year, a reverse gear was added to the transmission. Several prototypes with the Knucklehead motor and a Cardan drive to the rear wheel were produced for the army, but these had no chance against the Jeep. Beginning in 1967, the box was made with integral plastic fenders. With the introduction of the W motor in 1937, the ServiCar also received the new 45-cubic-inch power plant and retained it until the 1970s. Thanks to the ServiCar, the W series of motors remained in production far longer than any other power plant in the history of Harley-Davidson to date: The side valve motors came off the Milwaukee production line for thirty-seven years. Production numbers were never sensational, but over the years—excluding the prewar and war years—annual production was almost always in excess of 1,000 machines. Long after the Flathead motor had

The large metal box offered plenty of space for tools and spare parts.

disappeared from Harley's two-wheelers, the side-valve machines were brought into the Twentieth Century. In 1964, the ServiCar became the very first Harley-Davidson to have an electric starter and a 12-Volt electrical system. Production of the ServiCar ended in 1973, when 425 were built. It had been in production for forty-one years! Examples from 1932, the first production year, are rare today, as are the last machines, which were fitted with disc brakes near the end of production. Surely this is an indication that the termination of production was not planned in advance—otherwise why would they have continued development of the model for the next generation of brakes? Since then there have been no more commercial three-wheelers—and the police once again have to fill out their tickets standing up ...

As on two-wheel machines, the shifter was positioned on the left side of the tank.

Left: View of the tank and steering head— the motor frame was identical to that of the motorcycle.

Right: The rear drum brake could be locked, so that the three-wheeler could be parked on a slope.

Front view: The Servi-Car attracted attention wherever it went.

Below: Perfectly restored, this Servi-Car is a real museum piece.

Technical Data
SERVICAR G (1932)

Frame:	Double loop steel tube frame, rigid auxiliary frame with sprung metal box
Fork:	Springer
Motor:	Air-cooled V2, side valve control, chain drive, battery coil ignition, 3-speed manual transmission
Cylinders:	2, 45° cylinder angle
Displacement:	45.26 cubic inches
Output:	18 hp
Construction Year:	1932-1972

VLD (1933)
Art Nouveau Flatheads

Scarcely four years after the start of the world economic crisis, Harley-Davidson found itself in probably the deepest hole in the company's history. The motorcycle market in the USA was at rock bottom. Although Harley had only one competitor in the country in Indian, it was unable to make any capital from the situation. Sales had dropped seventy percent compared to 1929. The unemployed had other worries than buying new motorcycles. The outlook was poor, and even business people postponed purchasing a motorcycle or picked up a cheap used machine made by one of the now bankrupt manufacturers. The VL (886 examples) and the VLD

A real gem of Art Déco design: Harley-Davidson launched a new era with the VLD.

(780) were by far the most produced models in 1933. It was fortunate for the company that the V-series motors had been developed before the crisis. It had a solid power plant for its machines and all that was required was to adapt their appearance to meet the desires of its customers. In short: The market for olive green motorcycles was sated.

In 1930, the V-series had replaced the two cam J and JD models. The engines' combustion chambers had been designed by Harry Ricardo, the reigning "Pope of motorcycles," to optimize combustion and performance. The motors, now with side valves, could be equipped with pistons of different

heights in order to vary performance. The VLD, or Sport Solo, was the top of the line model and, in addition to high compression, it was given special lightweight pistons made of an aluminum-magnesium alloy. A Linkert M-21 carburetor was mounted on the Y manifold for fuel atomization.

When it came to paint finish, the company made a complete change in its policy, undoubtedly in an effort to improve sales. For the first time in the firm's history, Harley-Davidson offered a variety of basic finishes at no extra cost. The eagle on the tank also gave the motorcycle a new motif in the popular Art Déco style. The step countered Indian's colorful bikes, but the competitor from Springfield, Massachusetts was owned by the DuPont family and had direct access to the best paints in the world. Harley-Davidson countered with Silver-Turquoise, Black-Mandarin Red, Sunshine Blue-White, Police Blue-White, and Brilliant Green-Olive—all with elaborate pinstripes, which then were still applied by hand. Harley-Davidson was determined to draw attention to its bikes through the use of bright colors.

In 1933, motorcycle racing was still a sport that demanded the rider's full attention: foot clutch, hand shift, timing adjustment, and the roads—which in Europe and the USA were still better suited to trucks and horse-drawn carts than motorcycles. Only with a sidecar could one drift with relative ease over the roads, which were frequently covered in ruts, especially when it rained. And this did not just apply to the unpaved country roads between towns: Anyone who has driven a modern two-wheeler over cobblestones can empathize a little with the problems faced by the Harley rider of 1933. In the press and among riders, at least, the VL series received enthusiastic approval. The clutch engaged positively and shifting the three-speed transmission was simple. One engaged the foot clutch and shifted into first gear, which was something of a feat, especially on a slope, if one had to simultaneously brake with the left hand. The foot brake was unavailable as the right foot was holding up the bike. The rider then carefully opened the throttle while gently releasing the clutch and the motorcycle began to move. After a few meters he could shift into second and third gear. After setting

The heart of the bike: the 47-cubic-inch side-valve motor.

Left: More air inlet than filter.

Right: Polished to a high gloss; hand shifter.

the ignition timing, the rider was free to enjoy the passing scenery. With its high compression, the VLD developed a little more than 32 hp, and with its impressive torque the engine readily accepted lazy shifting. With the drum brakes of the time, the watchword was "keep an eye out ahead while driving"—there were more than enough obstacles.

Not until the 1934 model year did Harley-Davidson switch from the loss oil principle to dry sump lubrication. The hand pump for additional lubrication was retained, however, for difficult road and riding conditions and riding at top speed. Throughout its production life, the VL series underwent a continuous modification and improvement process.

One small historical anecdote concerning the VL series motorcycles comes from the confusion of the Spanish Civil War of 1936-1939, when a 1933 Harley-Davidson VL motorcycle saw action during the siege of the Alcazar. The besieged troops had removed the bike's rear wheel and ran the motor nonstop to generate electricity until Franco's troops forced them to surrender. It was already becoming apparent that the olive green color would soon be needed again ...

Left: The small tail light with external cable.

Right: Left side rearview mirror.

Complex instruments distributed on the tank.

Below: The graphic eagle heralded in a period of stylish designs, from which the company history draws to this day.

Technical Data
VLD (1933)

Frame:	Double loop steel tube, rigid
Fork:	Springer fork
Motor:	Air-cooled V2, side valve control, chain drive, battery coil ignition, 3-speed manual transmission
Cylinders:	2, 45° cylinder angle
Displacement:	74.21 cubic inches
Output:	approximately 32 hp
Construction Year:	1933-1936

EL 61 OHV (1936)
The First Knucklehead

Although Harley-Davidson had suffered badly as a result of the 1929 stock market crash, it never ceased to offer new models. Nevertheless, in 1933 sales figures fell to 3,700 motorcycles. Harley's competitors were in no better shape, however.

Harley-Davidson began working on a new, more modern motor, which was a brave decision in difficult times. As well, new machines had to be procured for its production, which was not easy in those lean times, but which was to pay off handsomely. The priority was to strive for technical innovation, and the company succeeded. In the first year of Knucklehead production alone, 1,678 motorcycles were made, and

Harley-Davidson's fortunes began to rise again. Sales were divided between the Model E with medium compression and 37 hp and the Model EL with higher compression and 40 hp. Development of the Knucklehead OHV motor, so-called because the shape of the rocker boxes resembled knuckles, began in the economically-difficult year of 1933. Racer Joe Petrali helped with development and, naturally, he placed much emphasis on performance and reliability.

The 61-cubic-inch motor—equivalent to just under 1000 cc—was produced to international standards, like many other motors with the same displacement. The engine entered

A classic on two wheels: the Harley-Davidson EL of 1936.

production in 1935, and with it the EL had a full 10 hp more than its predecessor, making it a very fast, responsive motorcycle. The EL achieved an unbelievable 95 miles per hour (153 kilometers per hour), enabling it to leave its 1000 cc competitors far behind. The motor had just one camshaft which operated four cams, and it was lighter and, more importantly, quieter than its predecessor. The modern power plant had dry sump lubrication with a separate oil tank over the gearbox, which was to become an often-copied trademark of V-Twins from Milwaukee. The motor was supplied by a speed-dependent oil pump, which produced greater oil pressure at low revolutions. The overhead valve motor was controlled by pushrods and rockers, but unfortunately, in the first year there were problems with oil supply and leaks. These were largely overcome in 1936, however.

With its gleaming engine parts, the Knuckle was, and still is today, a visually impressive motor, which was built in a similar technical configuration until the introduction of the EVO. With good treatment, it is a true friend for life, which is evidenced by the large number of these bikes still in existence. Harley-Davidson developed several innovations around the motor

The Springer fork is equipped with springs and damping.

Left: The foot-operated "Suicide Clutch" is more than just a nickname.

Right: Real work—four gears are now shifted by hand.

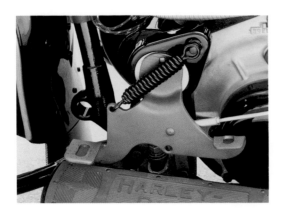

for the EL 61. A new clutch was introduced which considerably eased shifting of the four-speed transmission. The clutch was operated by the left foot, which earned it the name "suicide clutch." The carburetor was a 1.25-inch (32-mm) Linkert unit.

The motor was also a starting point for the design of a new motor meant to appeal to more sporting bikers. A new frame was developed, with two bearers for the motor. It was a rigid frame with a springer fork and a very comfortable single seat, which was of course sprung. The factory also completely redesigned the braking system, and beginning with the 1936 model year the motorcycle had larger and better adjustable drum brakes front and rear.

The E and EL models were also given a new speedometer with a white face, and in 1937 an odometer was added. The chassis, which rode on 18-inch wheels, had a two-piece folding rear fender, to make it easier to change the spoked wheel. Both models had a price of $380, which was undoubtedly why significantly more higher-performance EL models were sold. Racer Joe Petrali, who had taken part in its development, confirmed the motorcycle's great potential. At Daytona Beach, in 1937, he set a world speed record with the EL 61, achieving 136.2 miles per hour. After five production years, the bike's performance was raised again when Harley-Davidson introduced the 1200 cc Knucklehead motor to the market. Even today, to many, it is still the epitome of a Harley engine.

Left: The front drum brake.

Right: A classic to this day—the chromed horn of 1936.

The streamlined shape caught on: The 1936 Knucklehead reflected the style of the time.

Left: Front view—the fenders are still three times as wide as the tires.

Technical Data
EL 61 OHV (1936)

Frame:	Double loop steel tube, rigid
Fork:	Springer fork
Motor:	Air-cooled V2 Knucklehead, OHV control, chain drive, battery coil ignition, 4-speed manual transmission
Cylinders:	2, 45° cylinder angle
Displacement:	74 cubic inches
Output:	approximately 40 hp
Construction Year:	1936-1947

MODEL U "POLICE" (1937)
Law and Order on Two Wheels

In 1909, motorcycles began replacing horses as a means of transportation for the guardians of the law. Significantly, the Pittsburgh Police Authority selected the "Silent Gray Fellow" by Harley-Davidson to equip its units—and thus began a tradition. The big twins are still offered as police versions to this day, and Harley-Davidson test rides in the USA always offer rides for policemen on an actual basic Police model. Harley-Davidson police and escort vehicles had always been prestige objects, and in addition to the Shah of Persia, many justly and unjustly crowned leaders bet on police motorcycles from Milwaukee. By the middle of the 1930s, Harley-Davidson police motorcycles were being used in Shanghai, Rotterdam, Columbia, and Canada. In poor economic times when civilian sales were low, sales to the guardians of the law were a solid basis—and competition among the manufacturers was fierce, in particular because police use added a certain degree of prestige to the maker's name. As well, once a force had selected a brand of motorcycle, it was likely that it would return to the same source for future acquisitions.

Harley-Davidson offered the latest special equipment for its police machines, such as front wheel stands, extra headlights for pursuit and the illumination of crime scenes, fire

Modern equipment in 1937: the Model U with radio receiver.

extinguishers and later flashing lights, radios, and walkie-talkies. Exposed to wind and weather, on the contemporary roads—and, not least, at the mercy of the pitfalls of technology—police patrol duty was no bed of roses. Many law breakers were able to get away. A policeman of the 1930s recalled: "If the machine didn't start after the second or third kick, one could simply allow the speeder to drive on; and if I drove 10,000 miles, I must have run another 5,000 chasing my cap …"

During the Depression in the early 1930s, there was another factor: The criminals had outstripped the police in technical matters. Autos with V8 engines could do 80 miles an hour on the streets despite weighing several tons. The uncontrolled spread of Thompson submachine guns also gave the lawbreakers superior firepower. The typical police officer had just a six-shot Colt in his holster, and while driving, a motorcycle policeman could only fire if he was left-handed, for the Harley-Davidson's throttle was on the right.

In 1933 and 1934, the USA declared war on crime and armed the FBI, which until then had only been responsible for interstate crimes and economic criminality. The motorcycle policemen found themselves in the very front lines against Dillinger, Al Capone, and the bank robbers who were everywhere according to the press.

The motorcycle makers also made improvements in performance: One year after the Knucklehead, which was simply too expensive for many communities during the economic crisis, Harley-Davidson unveiled a completely new side-valve motor: the U Model. The motor, which had a displacement of 80 cubic inches, was installed in the E chassis and also used the Knucklehead's tank and sheet metal parts. The modern-looking motor had a sealed oil circulation system, and its high torque made the machine especially popular among sidecar combination riders. It was ideally suited, therefore, to bearing the heavy police equipment.

While motorcycle policemen in the early Twentieth Century used emergency call boxes to stay in touch with their stations, at the end of

Left: Searchlight—for crime scenes and pursuit.

Right: The hand shifter was mounted on the round tank's flank.

the 1920s, the first tube radios for squad cars appeared on the market. Harley-Davidson offered the first radio receivers in the 1935 model year. The speaker was mounted on the handlebars and looked like a reversed headlight. The box with the tube receiver was located on the back. Those with a knowledge of vacuum tubes and their sensitivity to vibration are still amazed that the system functioned at all. It had a receiver only, and the officer could only receive orders and clues—which, on a motorcycle, was not always that simple. In 1938, Harley used the advertising slogan "Get set for greater traffic safety" for the U. It also showed the main activity of the motorcycle cop: chasing traffic violators. The cable-operated sirens used in those days are still a popular accessory, and not just for police motorcycle fans.

The Model U was built in a number of variants until 1948 and was offered for police use. During the war years civilian production did not come to a complete halt. By then more than 3,500 police departments were using Harley-Davidson motorcycles and of course replacements were needed. With the arrival of the Panhead in 1948, the days of side-valve motors in solo police motorcycles came to an end. Today, all U models are prized collectors' items, but police models are especially difficult to find. Original accessories, in particular, make these bikes real treasures.

Left: The vacuum tube receiver on the baggage carrier was fully exposed to vibration.

Right: Additional tail lights under the seat.

Modern mounting—instruments and lights are now integrated.

Below: Dressed up—no police officer would have ridden with this license plate holder.

Technical Data
MODEL U "POLICE" (1937-1948)

Frame:	Double loop steel tube, rigid
Fork:	Springer
Motor:	Air-cooled V2, side valve control, chain drive, battery coil ignition, 4-speed manual transmission
Cylinders:	2, 45° cylinder angle
Displacement:	74 cubic inches
Output:	approximately 30 hp
Construction Year:	1937-1948

XA 1000 (1942)
The Harley Boxer

Too late, too heavy, too expensive: Harley-Davidson's military motorcycle was justifiably rejected by the armed forces.

The XA 1000 was developed at the request of the US Army. Although America did not enter the war until the attack on Pearl Harbor in December 1941, preparations for war had been under way for years: New types of aircraft, tanks, vehicles and motorcycles were developed. The two remaining major motorcycle makers in the USA, Harley-Davidson and Indian, both modified their production vehicles for military use. Even before America's entry into the war, both companies delivered motorcycle to warring nations such as England and France. A shipment of 4,000 Indian Scouts for the French military is still lying on the bottom of the Bay of Biscay, victims of a German submarine. The US Army was particularly impressed by the German motorcycle-sidecar combinations with boxer engines produced by BMW and Zündapp, which were employed with success by motorized units during the campaigns in Poland and France. In 1941, the motorcycle units' field of operations was expanded to include Russia and North Africa. We will probably never know to what extent the Americans were taken in by propaganda master Goebbels' newsreels, in which the telegenic motorcycle troops often figured. Both Harley-Davidson and Indian received an order for 1,000 pre-production prototypes with Cardan shaft drives. While Indian's

BMW copy: The XA's horizontally-opposed motor was later used as a stationary motor.

solution used many proven components of the Sport Scout—the engine was in fact an 841 turned through 90 degrees. Harley-Davidson copied the German original, which proved to be a mistake. In North Africa, British troops had captured a number of BMW R 75 sidecar motorcycles, and it was this, along with the Zündapp KS 750, that was to be recreated. How this machine ultimately changed into a BMW R 11, whose design was already ten years old, while on its way to the army proving center has never been fully explained—yet Harley-Davidson faithfully copied the German "old timer" without questioning why. The German bike's metric measurements were converted into inches, and the four-speed gearbox had a foot shifter. The double loop tubular frame with rigid plate spring rear suspension was derived from that of BMW; however, by the end of the war, it had been replaced by the rigid unit from the WLA. By American standards, the XA was a modern motorcycle, even though it was based on a design already ten

years old. Side-controlled valves were state of the art and were unchanged from the Knucklehead of 1936. The 738 cc motor produced 23 hp at 4,600 rpm. For a motorcycle weighing 536.8 pounds (244 kilograms), this was hardly sufficient to deliver sparkling performance. The quadratic bore-stroke ratio was $3\frac{1}{16}$ inches with a compression ration of 5.7:1. As with the BMW, the oil circulation system was integrated in the motor, which made an oil tank superfluous. The two-part fuel tank had a capacity of a little over two gallons. Despite the fact that 1,000 examples were made, sometimes under the confusing designation XA 1000, the XA never got beyond the testing stage. The motorcycle was tested by armored and cavalry troops in Fort Knox where, in addition to the gold reserves of the United States, there is a large barrack housing a museum. Both disc and spoked wheels were tested during trials, but by then, the US Army had decided in favor of the Jeep. The army had also come to the conclusion that simultaneously driving

Left and right: The rifle scabbard covered the additional shock absorber.

a motorcycle and firing a weapon was almost impossible—while in a Jeep one soldier steered and three others could use their weapons. Harley-Davidson also took part in the Jeep competition with an air-cooled horizontally-opposed motor, but was not awarded a contract. The boxer motor had its chance, fitted with an electrical generator unit.

Though expected by many, after the war Harley-Davidson did not offer a civilian version of the XA—management probably still remembered the failure of the Model W sport twins in 1919. Installed longitudinally, the boxer motor was anything but a sales hit. Some historians have written that Harley-Davidson tested a prototype with a telescopic fork and modern overhead valve cylinder heads in 1946, but then discarded the design. It must be kept in mind that, by 1945, the technology of the XA was already fifteen years old. After the war, the surviving XA models were sold to private interests for $500 apiece. Because of this, many civilian and military versions may be seen at vintage motorcycle and military vehicle gatherings.

Instrumentation came from the FLA.

Left: The tail lights were shielded.

Right: Main headlight, horn and the small driving light for traveling under combat conditions.

Fully equipped and with disc wheels: a perfectly restored XA.

Left: The lubrication instructions screwed onto the frame.

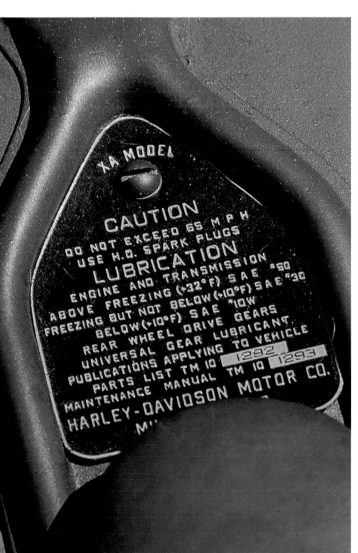

Technical Data
XA 1000 (1942)

Frame:	Double loop steel tube, rigid
Fork:	Springer fork with additional shock absorbers
Motor:	Air-cooled, two-cylinder horizontally-opposed, OHV, shaft drive, 4 speed manual transmission
Cylinders:	2, 180° cylinder angle
Displacement:	738 ccm
Output:	approximately 23 hp
Construction Year:	1942

WLA (1942)
The Motorcycle That
(Almost) Won the War

The warhorse for the Second World War: The WLA was used on every front as a communications vehicle and also by the military police.

Harley-Davidson was probably not fond of hearing that the motorcycle was not a decisive weapon of war. Not in the First World War, when British, French, and German troops mounted machine-guns on the sidecars of the first motorcycles, some of then even armored; and also not in the Second World War, when the Wehrmacht's motorcycle troops supported the panzer units, but principally to provide a "good image" for the propaganda of the weekly newsreels.

When the Americans entered the war on 7 December 1941, American planners still had images of fast motorized Huns in their memories, explaining the huge orders placed with the two major manufacturers of motorcycles that had survived the Depression, Harley-Davidson and Indian. In reality, the motorcycle's value as a fighting machine was extremely suspect, for even experienced riders had their hands (and feet!) full just driving the machine.

One can imagine the fantastic scene of a wild horde of Harley riders shooting out of the landing craft and thundering up the beach. German machine-guns would have put an end to any such charge before the sea wall that barred the entire length of Omaha Beach in Normandy. In fact, during the Second World War, there was neither a famous photo—like Ray Holtz's "The first Harley entering Germany" in

Robust and reliable:
Anyone could quickly
make friends with the
WLA's 741-cc side-
valve motor.

November 1918—nor any noteworthy stories of Harley-Davidson motorcycles in combat. All of the action photos that appeared in **Harley-Davidson Enthusiast** magazine were posed—luckily for the soldiers, as the metal skid plate under the motor was not armor steel. One can easily assess the wisdom of taking cover from enemy fire behind the gas tank.

The motorcycle was a kind of workhorse: When used as a courier or patrol vehicle, the WLA could exploit its best feature, its maneuverability. One chapter of the war that has never been described is the direction of supply traffic from Normandy to the evermore distant front lines from August 1944. The supply trucks were controlled exclusively by MPs on their Harley-Davidson WLAs, day and night and in sun, rain, and snow.

Although the WLA first appears in the production statistics in the 1941 model year, when 2,282 were built, there had already been pre-production and test machines, which the US Army tested at Fort Knox. Conscious that war

was coming, Harley-Davidson began war production in November 1938—just after the Munich Agreement and Hitler's last peaceful coup. The first two prototypes of the WLA were handed over to the Mechanized Cavalry Board in August 1939. In addition to high-gloss paint, they had many chrome parts—after all, they weren't in the war yet. The WLA had the WL's 738 cc (45-cubic-inch) motor with lowered compression ration and larger cooling fins, as the machine would mostly be operated at low speeds. As well, the gears of the manual three-speed transmission were adjusted for military use. With a power plant producing just 23 hp at 4,600 rpm, with military equipment—rifle sheath, touring screen, saddlebags, ammunition box, roll bar, and a sturdy baggage carrier—the WLA was underpowered. With just the basic equipment this workhorse weighed 572 pounds (260 kilograms)! The headlight had special shields to conceal it from the air, and the rear lights were doubled for safety. The fenders were extra wide to cope

From top to bottom: The air filter box made it easier to ford streams.

Hand shifter on the tank.

A sturdy baggage carrier.

with accruing mud. The US Army imposed stringent requirements for a deep wading capability, consequently a special air filter box was installed under the seat. A longer intake manifold and the filter also reduced performance. All in all, the machine lived up to its robust exterior and proved itself in every theater of war in Europe and in the Pacific. When America entered the war in 1941, Harley-Davidson introduced round the clock, three-shift production. An almost identical model, the WLC (C for Canada) was built for the Canadian Army. Altogether 88,000 WLA motorcycles left the production lines in Milwaukee—and another 30,000 were built as spare parts and not assembled. Even today, it is possible to buy original WLA spare parts still wrapped in wax paper at old-timer markets and from specialist dealers. More than sixty years after the end of the Second World War, the spare parts supply for this Harley is assured for years to come.

Left: The small driving light on the fender provided little illumination.

Right: Double tail lights for improved safety while driving in a column.

The WLA profited from Harley-Davidson's experience with poor road conditions: A low center of gravity allowed for good handling.

Below: View from the seat—which way to the front please?

Technical Data
WLA (1942)

Frame:	Single loop steel tube, rigid
Fork:	Springer
Motor:	Air-cooled V2, side valve control, chain drive, battery coil ignition, 3-speed manual transmission
Cylinders:	2, 45° cylinder angle
Displacement:	45.26 cubic inches
Output:	approximately 23.5 hp
Construction Year:	1941-1945

SPORTSTER (1957)
Sportiness and Design for Generations...

The Harley-Davidson Sportster probably has the longest production life in motorcycle history. In 1957, it replaced the unpopular K model and began its triumphal march around the world. At a time when youth was discovering its freedom, American enthusiasm for motorsports was also growing. Motorcycle drag racing became an effective marketing tool. The Sportster fit into this trend when it arrived on the market, and with its 55 cubic inch (ca. 850 cc) motor, it was adequately powered for the day. The motor was a rough runner, but Harley had developed the OHV motor to go fast, not to win a prize for the quietest motor. With a compression ration of 7.5:1 and a bore-stroke ratio of 3 x

Plain and good looking: The XL Sportster was a great success in name and design.

3.812, the motor produced 55 hp and was a true sports motor with plenty of torque. The bike enabled Harley to hold its English opponents in check on the racetrack. Technology was on the move in 1957: The Russians sent the Sputnik into orbit, the first commercial atomic reactor was put into service, and the "Sporty" made its own modest contribution. The Model XL, a name that is still used today, had a modern power plant and weighed just over 440 pounds (200 kilograms), which for the time, and especially for Harley-Davidson, was quite low. The chassis and brake system were somewhat overtaxed by the sensational 55 hp,

but that was of little concern to the youthful and sport-oriented customers who purchased most of these machines. The chassis' weaknesses only became apparent in the upper speed range, which is normally not relevant for American conditions, and as we know, many modifications were made for racing use.

The concept of placing the motor and transmission, including primary drive, in one casing had proved itself, and this gave the Sportster additional stiffness in the frame. It also made possible a very compact design, which has been retained to the present day. As the motor was bolted rigidly to the frame, all of its vibrations were transmitted directly to the rider, but that too could be interpreted as pure motorcycling. The bike rode on 18-inch wheels and was equipped with two drum brakes, which was only changed much later. The V-Twin OHV motor remained a feature of the Sportster for many years and still resembles the original power plant of 1957, although the motor's inner workings have been steadily developed. Not until 1987 was the basic concept changed, when a redesigned aluminum motor was introduced. It was built until 2003, when the model was updated. The

history of the Sportster includes a number of extremely sporty models which were very successful, even on the racetrack. The legendary XR 750 dominated the flat track and dirt track races until the early 1990s. Even stunt riders, like Evel Knievel, relied on the sport bike from Milwaukee, with which he gave countless shows and also broke various records. In 1958, one year after the arrival of the XL series, Jack Heller raised the world speed record to 134.8 miles per hour on a salt lake. Even today, the Sportster is a popular dragster motorcycle, taking part in and winning quarter-mile races all over the world. The XR 1000, derived from the racetrack, with two large carburetors and 80 hp, was another demonstration of the development department's ambition to reach a new market, even though this never succeeded to the hoped-for degree. Instead, the Sportster was sold as the single-seater of the Harley family or as a "woman's motorcycle." The marketing department of course seized this and created models such as the Hugger which, with its shorter suspension was suitable for both male and female riders who otherwise had problems with the Sportster's rather tall design. The Sportster was not just popular with

Compact design: The Sportster's 45° V-Twin made optimal use of the available room inside the frame.

Left and right: Cleaner look—the front and rear drum brakes dispensed with looks in favor of cooling outer surfaces.

motorcycle racers. Impressed by the bike, Elvis Presley bought one and was often photographed on it. If one believes the museums and Hard Rock Cafés of this world, the **King of Rock 'n' Roll** must have owned at least twenty of these machines at one time, for so many Elvis bikes may be seen worldwide that they could never have all fit into the garage at Graceland.

That the basic shape of the Sportster is still recognizable today is a testament to the success of its designer. For what vehicle, apart from the Porsche 911 and the Sportster, has retained the original design basics of the first model?

Left: A lot of chrome and the tachometer in the fork fairing.

Right: Design classic—Sportster shock absorber.

A beauty even by today's standards—and at 495 pounds (225 kilograms) astonishingly light in weight.

Below: Another part for the Harley legend—the horn.

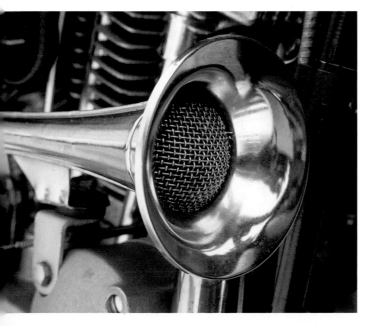

Technical Data
XL SPORTSTER (1957)

Frame:	Double loop steel tube, rigid, steel tube swing arm, 2 shock absorbers
Fork:	Telescopic
Motor:	Air-cooled V2 Ironhead Sportster, OHV control, chain drive, 4-speed manual transmission
Cylinders:	2, 45° cylinder angle
Displacement:	53.87 cubic inches
Output:	approximately 40 hp
Construction Year:	1957-1959

[71]

DUO GLIDE (1964)
The Company Flagship

A Harley-Davidson advertising brochure from the late Fifties declared: "Three-point damping brings motorcycle riding into a new dimension." The rear, hydraulically-activated drum brake was also touted as a technical revolution. Scarcely imaginable today, but when production of the Duo Glide began, this was a true milestone for Harley-Davidson. The first Duo Glide models were produced by the Motor Company in 1958 and became the embodiment of comfortable motorcycle riding.

The motorcycle remained part of the program until 1964 and approximately 37,000 of all versions were sold. It was a time when Rock 'n' Roll was heading toward its heyday, the pace of technological advancement was constantly rising, and the road cruisers in the USA were becoming ever larger. Huge tail fins adorned the side parts of automobiles, girls discovered the petticoat, the church warned people about the dangers of "Negro music," and the unhealthy effects of the *Twist*. Everything in best order, therefore. Even a certain Elvis Presley, who began his unbelievable career in the late 1950s, was a Harley fan, although, as mentioned, the actual number of Duo Glides he owned in addition to countless street cruisers is difficult to ascertain. Yet, just as the music of the young, hip-swinging rebels defined an era, the Duo

Road cruiser on two wheels: The Duo Glide is true American baroque.

Chrome-laden—there must be room for one more accessory somewhere.

Glide represented a milestone in the history of Harley-Davidson. Sometimes one hears a modern hit song that was clearly influenced by Rock 'n' Roll; and if one looks at the Heritage Softail, its strong resemblance to the Duo Glide is immediately obvious.

The motorcycle was equipped with a modified Panhead motor which was constantly upgraded as production went on. In the FLH version, thanks to higher compression and a reinforced camshaft, the 1200 cc motor produced a solid 60 hp. Because of the motorcycle's lavish equipment, this extra power was needed to achieve acceptable performance. In the end, the Duo Glide was probably the most powerful bike in the world in its day. Given the bike's weight, it was not just enough to just increase power, and so the technicians set about improving cooling as well. For improved motor cooling, the rocker

boxes were made of solid material and cooling ribs were added to the rocker covers. Over the years, the motor underwent various modifications, such as strengthened rockers, a modified kick starter, single ignition with one ignition coil per cylinder and endless optical modifications. The motorcycle had a two-in-one exhaust system, with a twin pipe system available as an option. Of course, the so-called Fishtail mufflers, which typified the look of the bike, were obligatory and even today are still installed by Harley fans.

The Duo Glide got its name from the design of its frame with two shock absorbers on the rear wheel swing arm. In keeping with the exuberant design of the motorcycle, these were enclosed in chrome covers. Harley didn't spare the chrome, and even the tool box, the primary cover, and many components were chromed. A new fork bridge, a new oil tank, and a

Left: Fragile—
nevertheless this
wheel mounting had
to carry 770 pounds
(350 kilograms).

Right: 1964—the
last year with a
kick starter.

Left: Main and
auxiliary headlights
provided good
illumination.

Right: Chrome
on the handlebars
and fittings.

modified swing arm had to be designed
for the new frame, so that one could say
that this was an entirely new motorcycle.
Drum brakes were still used, but the rear
brake was hydraulically actuated, which
better regulated braking power. All of this
also impressed the police and, in 1960, the
Milwaukee Police received new Duo Glides
and Servi-Cars from Harley-Davidson.

In 1960, the Motor Company
acquired fifty percent of the Italian
motorcycle manufacturer Aermacchi,
in order to be able to offer small-
displacement bikes and scooters. In
1962, the Company also acquired
an interest in the Tomahawk Boat
Company, which, in addition to
boats and golf carts, also produced
windshields, saddlebags, etc.

More angular design
on the tank dash and
steering head fairing.

Below: The classic
legend, in chrome
of course.

Technical Data
DUO GLIDE (1964)

Frame:	Double loop steel tube frame, steel tube swing arm, 2 shock absorbers
Fork:	Telescopic
Motor:	Air-cooled V2 Panhead, OHV control, chain drive, battery coil ignition, 4-speed manual transmission
Cylinders:	2, 45° cylinder angle
Displacement:	74 cubic inches
Output:	approximately 60 hp
Construction Year:	1958-1964

ELECTRA GLIDE (1965)
Igniting the Electric Spark...

The E-Glide, which appeared in 1965, was to be the last version with the Panhead motor, as the technical demands of the customers continued to grow. In production since 1948, the Panhead motor was no longer suitable for the heavier motorcycles Harley was making and was replaced during the course of E-Glide production. The Electra Glide, introduced in 1965, was to begin a new era in American motorcycle design. The fully equipped Full-Dresser bike was a touring model with every conceivable extra, but there were also problems. The legendary name Electra Glide was chosen by Harley-Davidson because it was the first model equipped with an electric starter. With every model change,

Pure Electra Glide: without the typical accessories like buddy seat and touring windscreen.

the motorcycle provided plenty of conversation material for the critics. The electric starter was sniggered at, as *real men* used a kick-starter to start their bikes ...

For the first two years, the motorcycle could be had with electric or kick starter, and in the former case, a cover was provided for the hole for the kick starter. The kick starter model was considerably lighter, and weight was also a problem for the E models.

The E-Glide was basically a developed version of the Duo Glide with a new frame. The early electric starters had their problems, for in the beginning they were poorly protected

against water, and there was often insufficient battery power to start the bike. And so the entire electrical system was reworked by the engineers and made watertight. The necessary changes added almost 88 pounds (40 kilograms) of weight. And it was not just the bike's performance that suffered: The braking system was no longer adequate, nor was the chassis. And so the technicians began tackling the various problems, the start of an unending tweaking process. The bike's weight took the frame to its limits and so it received additional stiffening to master the bike's unsettled driving characteristics. Weight could only be compensated for by additional power,

as the touring bike was now rather underpowered. The 1200 cc Panhead motor's compression was raised and additional camshaft lobes were installed; however, the modified motor ran very roughly and the camshaft bearings were unable to bear the load over the long term. And so the Motor Company decided to retire the Panhead motor and design a new one. The Shovelhead was born.

Admittedly the first series used a modified Panhead casing with stronger bearings and newly-designed, performance-optimized cylinder heads, but it all paid off. The motor again had the famous Harley-Davidson quality and was powerful enough for the 792

By 1965, the Panhead motor was exhausted, and in the years that followed, it would be developed further, step by step.

Still in the program
for traditionalists:
hand shifting.

Still in the program
for traditionalists:
hand shifting.

pound (360-kilogram) flagship of the company. Not until 1969 was the so-called Early Shovel replaced by the Late Shovel models.

Later examples, known as Alternator Shovel models, had a redesigned motor. The 1208 cc motor of the 1965 Electra Glide models produced 54 hp and had a four-speed transmission. There were two shifter versions, a hand shifter, recognizable by its small 14.2-liter fuel tank, and a foot shifter with a 19-liter tank. The motorcycle had a steel tube frame with telescoping swing arm and shock absorbers in the rear. It rode on 5 x 16 tires, which remained in use into modern times. The bike could be had

in a variety of finishes. Hifi-Blue and Hifi-Red were high-gloss colors which were offered in combination with white and resembled modern metallic paints. The motorcycle was equipped with twin-drum brakes and these too were frequently updated to provide sufficient braking power, even with touring accessories, which included a fiberglass luggage case and a buddy seat.

Following the initial changes to the motor, the chain drive was also modified to handle the increased power. In 1965, because of the many expensive innovations and growing competition from Japanese models on the American market, the Harley-Davidson Motor Company's capital base was very thin,

Left: Modern
primary casing.

Right: The rear drum
brake's hydraulic
fluid reservoir.

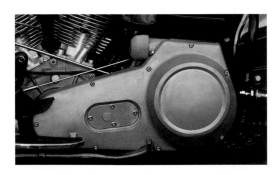

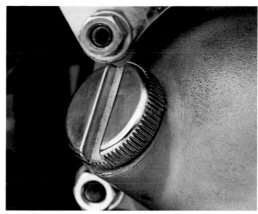

Left: Trip
odometer reset.

Right: Transmission
fluid filler screw.

and so the owners decided to go public.
The company was transformed into
a stock corporation, with the Harley
and Davidson families as majority
stockholders holding fifty-three percent
of the shares.

Below: The
massive battery.

Technical Data
ELECTRA GLIDE (1965)

Frame:	Double loop steel tube frame, steel tube swing arm, 2 shock absorbers
Fork:	Telescopic
Motor:	Air-cooled V2 Panhead, OHV control, chain drive, battery coil ignition, 4-speed manual transmission
Cylinders:	2, 45° cylinder angle
Displacement:	74 cubic inches
Output:	approximately 60 hp
Construction Year:	1965

XLCH SPORTSTER (1968)
Then Came Bronson...

The year 1968 was a time of change and hope: With the prospect of Apollo 11 landing on the moon anything seemed possible—and the "Summer of Love" was just one year in the past. The motorcycle as a spare time vehicle, as an attitude towards life, as an expression of independence and freedom—that was the new trend. And it wasn't only the Japanese who were offering appealing models that were easy to operate. In the past, motorcycles, in particular Harleys as used by outlaw clubs, served mainly as replacements for horses. The villains rode into towns to terrorize them—and at the proper moment, the horse went down so that the good guys could prevail. The *B*

movies of the late Sixties were full of chain-rattling, greasy bikes that one better not meet alone—an image that began to rub off on other Harley riders.

By 1968, the Sportster series had been in production for eleven years—a considerable duration for those times. Visually, it had remained more or less the same, but there had been significant technical improvements. In 1965, it received a 12-Volt electrical system, and in 1967, an electric starter. By 1968, such was the confidence in the electric starter that the kick starter was eliminated. At the same time, the model also received a new front fork.

Still a bit retro in design in 1968, but with modern technology: the 1968 Sportster.

The year 1968 was also significant because, for the first time, Harley-Davidson had to install a special exhaust system to meet the stiffer emission standards of one state: The "California Muffler" initiated a new calendar. Typically, only new machines had to be equipped with this exhaust. As before, after his purchase, the customer could equip his bike with the loud open pipes of his choice—which is what the majority did. It would be a miracle to find such a Sportster still in its original configuration. That model year also saw a further simplification of operation: The previous manual ignition advance during starting was replaced by an automatic system. This was also a tribute to better combustion and environmental protection, not to mention a safety factor for the mainly young riders of Sportster motorcycles,

who wanted nothing to do with the relics from the early days of motorcycling that had been in use for decades. The modification did nothing to hurt performance. Even with the "plugged" West Coast Muffler, the 882 cc V-Twin still produced 58 hp at 6,800 rpm.

The image of the Sportster was polished by races at the drag strip and at the Baja California: When he won at Daytona in 1968, Cal Rayborn was still riding a KRTT side-valve bike, but the XR 750 was still in testing. With that bike, Harley-Davidson would dominate the dirt tracks for the next decade.

Climb on, press the button, drive away—by 1969, the Sportster had become such a mature motorcycle that it received the "second leading role" in Michael Parks' television series **Then Came Bronson**. From episode to episode, Charles Bronson rode his "Ironhead"

Power plant: The 1968 Sportster's motor produced almost 50 hp; even more was possible in the hands of a skilled tuner.

The production tank was not very popular. During customization these were replaced with "peanut" tanks, which Harley itself would use before long.

Sportster to new adventures. There would be no better television advertising for Harley-Davidson until *Renegade*.

And Harley-Davidson badly needed the advertising: By 1968, the V-Twin program had shrunk to four FL and two XL models. Production figures were 1,650 units for the FL, 5,300 for the FLH, 1,975 for the XLH, and 4,900 for the XLCH. The company also made 600 GE Servi-Cars for police use, but these were still powered by the antiquated prewar side-valve motor. These were not exactly impressive figures in the core business of the motorcycle manufacturer; however, it should not be forgotten that production was strongly diversified at that time, and in addition to the big twins, the company also made large numbers of smaller bikes with 125 and 250 cc motors and offered 50 and 65 cc bikes as well as snowmobiles and golf carts. On 18 December 1968—in the middle of the 1969 model year—Harley-Davidson was taken over by American Machine and Foundry (AMF). A financial crisis had made the sale of Harley-Davidson necessary. For Harley-Davidson, too, this was a year of decision.

Left: Tachometer in a chrome housing on the forks.

Right: Additional ribs helped cool the motor housing.

On its way to becoming a chopper? The handlebars suited the public's taste.

The popularity of the Sportster in those days is obvious from the production figures—and it was to continue into the early Seventies. Not until 1971, when Willie G. Davidson trimmed the Super Glide with the Custom Look and melded the FLH frame with the optics of the Sportster, did the big twin models again gain ground. But the success story of the Sportster had just begun ...

Below: The headlamp sat deep in the fairing.

Technical Data
XLCH SPORTSTER (1968)

Frame:	Double loop steel tube frame, steel tube swing arm, 2 shock absorbers
Fork:	Telescopic
Motor:	Air-cooled V2 Ironhead, OHV control, chain drive, 4-speed manual transmission
Cylinders:	2, 45° cylinder angle
Displacement:	53.87 cubic inches
Output:	approximately 45 hp
Construction Year:	1958-1971

FL EARLY SHOVEL (1969)
A Bit of "Easy Rider"

The 1969 FL, a bike powered by the so-called Early Shovel motor, was produced in a year which unleashed an image change for the Motor Company and also saw mankind make a giant leap forward. With the words, "One small step for man, one giant leap for mankind," Neil Armstrong became the first man to set foot on the moon. Just twenty minutes later, Edwin Aldrin also left the landing craft and both names remain well-known today. Even trips to other planets appeared feasible and no longer pure vision. For others, there was the movie *Easy Rider*, which hit the theaters in 1969. Dennis Hopper and Peter Fonda are, today, symbols of the biker, and a little of each is in every motorcycle rider. The independence, cool custom bikes and, of course, the legendary clothes worn by the two main characters are an inherent part in the heads, many garages, and closets of the Harley community. Many bikers make copies of the *Captain America* and there are stories and rumors about the fate of the original, but who knows for sure? Of course, some blockheads still content that the moon landing was the most expensive film production of all time.

Basic version: Today, a true to the original 1969 FL is as rare as snow in the desert. Most fell prey to the early customization craze in the 1970s.

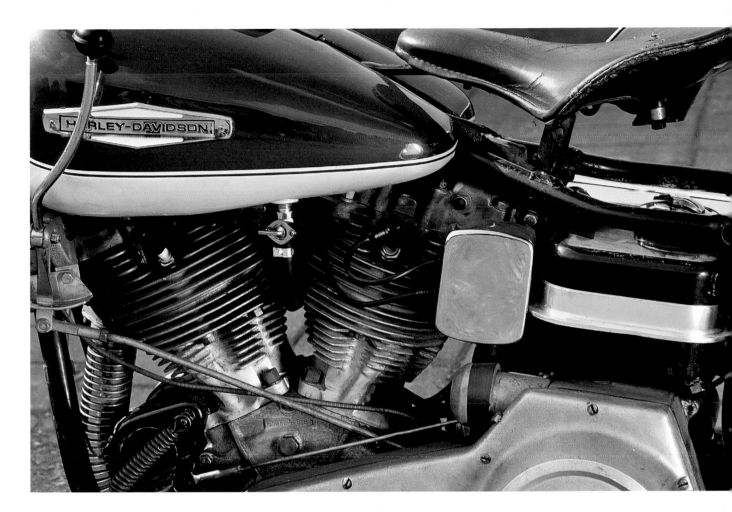

That same year, Harley-Davidson produced a bike that didn't really go with the movie; but who could suspect that the film production and these bikes would become an apparently never-ending cult. The rather radical 1969 FL was a so-called Early Shovel, which meant that the motor block was largely similar to that of the Panhead. Conversion to a 12-Volt electrical system made the bike a few kilograms heavier, so that more power was required. Newly-designed aluminum cylinder heads with increased compression and redesigned channels resulted in a solid ten-percent increase in output compared to the Panhead motor. The motor produced just under 60 hp, but that was enough to propel the bike to 100 miles per hour (160 kilometers per hour), which was absolutely adequate for the existing roads. The identifying feature of the motor was the valve covers, which followed the form of the Sportster motors and because of their "shovel shape" resulted in the name Shovelhead.

A completely redesigned motor capable of 66 hp was introduced in 1970. Weighing 781 pounds (355 kilograms), the 1969 model cost $1,900 and, with optional accessories, the price easily surpassed $2,000. The FL Electra Glide Super Solo, the version's complete title, could also be had as a police motorcycle, which further drove up not just the price, but the weight as well. At that time the 1,200 cc motor was equipped with battery coil ignition and was aspirated by a 38-mm Tillot carburetor. In contrast to its predecessors, the model was fitted with the Sportster XL's oval air filter to reduce exhaust emissions and noise. The suspension consisted of a telescopic fork at the front and a swing arm with two shock absorbers in the rear.

Cleaned up: The Shovelhead motor now produced around 60 hp.

[85]

Left: The drum brake in the rear hub was hydraulically activated.

Right: Inside the primary housing, a chain links the motor and transmission.

Braking power was still provided by two drum brakes, with the rear brake hydraulically activated. Beginning in 1972, the FL came with a front disc brake, to reduce stopping distance to an acceptable level. Much to the joy of the customers, the FL was fitted with an electric starter. To the tough guys, this and any other change aimed at simplifying operation of the motorcycle was regarded as unnecessary and for softies only. As we know, however, this innovation stuck, and the customers were spared many sore legs from kick-

starting. A hand or foot shifter could be had, but as we know the foot shifter won out as it made the bike easier to operate. The last models, the 1969s, are prized collectors' items today, in part because of the relatively small number of Early Shovels made. The Early Shovel motor remains a reliable power plant to this day, provided it receives proper servicing or is restored.

Left: "Vacuum Cleaner Hose," a nickname that has stuck.

Right: Still in demand—hand shifter. It was now mounted on the frame.

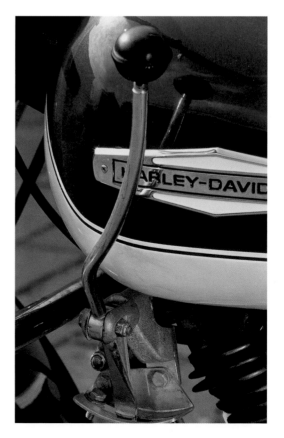

Two drum brakes still stopped the 770-pound (350-kilogram) package.

Below: The brake fluid reservoir for the rear brake.

Technical Data
FL EARLY SHOVEL (1969)

Frame:	Double loop steel tube frame, steel tube swing arm, 2 shock absorbers
Fork:	Telescopic fork
Motor:	Air-cooled V2 Shovelhead, OHV control, chain drive, battery coil ignition, 4-speed manual transmission, electric start
Cylinders:	2, 45° cylinder angle
Displacement:	74 cubic inches
Output:	approximately 60 hp
Construction Year:	1969

XLCR CAFÉ RACER (1977-1978)
...Good Bike, Bad Timing...

Anyone who learned to ride a moped or motorcycle in the 1970s will surely remember the top bikes of the time: Honda CB 750, Suzuki GT 750, Van Veen, Kawasaki Z 900, Yamaha XS 1100, BMW R 90 S, Ducati SS 750, Norton Commando, Harley-Davidson Electra Glide—and thus we have already explained part of the failure of Harley-Davidson's contemporary sports bike series.

Harley led all of its competitors in displacement, which very quickly resulted in the marque's international image becoming that of a "fat tub." Walter Villa's Grand Prix victories in the 250 cc and 350 cc race (Villa was world champion in the 350 cc class in 1977) did nothing to change this.

The Sportster had been a solid fixture in Harley-Davidson's lineup since 1957—the 1000 cc V-Twin combined a solid performance and low weight. Thanks to its four cam lobes, the engine was loved by mechanics: For the drag strip, it was possible to coax significantly more performance from the Sportster's motor than from those of the big-displacement twins. The XLCR was a design work of Willie G. Davidson, who produced an absolute masterpiece of Café Racer styling. Based on the XL production model, the great-grandson of the company founder gave the bike a new tank, exhaust system, twin disc brake sup front, one-man bench seat and numerous optical details,

Modern look, even by today's standards: The XLCR is still a real treat.

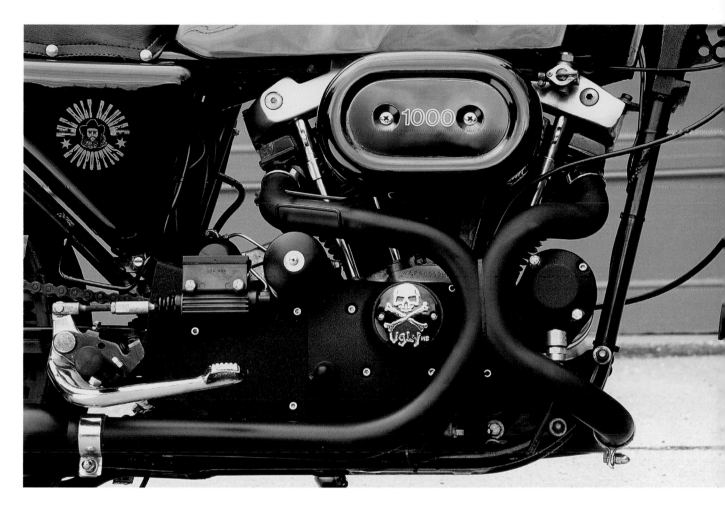

such as the narrow sports handlebars. The only addition to the sport version of the motor was an oil cooler, and the frame was specially designed for the XLCR: The rear frame triangle enclosed the oil tank and allowed the shock absorbers to be mounted almost vertically. The rear part of the bike was reminiscent of contemporary inspirations and competitors like the Norton Commando Fastback, the Kawasaki tailpiece or Willie G's boat tail for the Sportster and FX models of 1970. Naturally, it most strongly resembles the sport tail of Harley's own XR 750 dirt track models. The fairing and tail section were made of fiberglass, while the Morris cast aluminum wheels were among the most modern motorcycle wheels available in 1977.

The black coloring was a total departure from the brightly-colored production series models—to say nothing of the creations that the custom scene produced for bike shows in the 1970s: Shiny plastic parts contrasted with the matt-black 2-in-2 exhaust pipe whose curved sections were welded together beneath the air filter. Motor casing, cylinders, alternator, and transmission cover were given a black textured paint finish for better heat dissipation, which caused the polished components such as cylinder heads, push rods, forks, and hubs to stand out even more. The XLCR was, and is, a delight to the eye—and it remains a mystery why the machine stayed a shelf warmer.

With its four-speed transmission and weight of just over 473 pounds (215 kilograms), the Café Racer was definitely capable of sporting performance, though not without considerable vibration development. The 1000 Sportster motor, however, produced just 55 hp, which was just too little compared to the Japanese four-cylinders and also the British and

A visual treat, the Ironhead was incapable of true performance. The exhaust system with welded, curved pipes was only available on this model.

Left: Exhaust pipe very close to the motor.

Right: Speedometer and tachometer in the handlebar fairing.

Italian twins. A BMW R 90 S—similar in displacement and style—delivered 70 hp at the rear wheel.

There were 1,923 examples of the Café Racer built in 1977 and just 1,201 in 1978.

The XLCR could be had with the optional two-person bench seat—but it was not any lack of togetherness that was responsible for its failure to sell. When seen against the 30,000 1977-1978 XL models that were produced, there just weren't enough weekend racers to justify keeping the series in production.

At first, the XLCR was a shelf-warmer, but as time went on, it became a collectors' item. There has never been an absence of customers seeking café racer versions of later Sportsters—but these conversions never reached significant numbers.

While the 1000 Ironhead Sportster is no rarity, today it is difficult to find true to the original XLCRs: Neither the chassis nor the body parts were ever used in another Harley-Davidson model. Anyone who can cruise past the ice cream parlor on a true to the original restored XLCR is sure to attract looks. And even the hard-bitten big twin drivers go into raptures about the "old days." Perhaps, if more of them had bought one back then, there might be more of the machines around today.

Left: Modern control elements.

Right: The tail end of the dirt track race bikes.

Willie G.'s masterpiece: slim lines and modern technology.

Below: Aerodynamically refined—except for the mirrors.

Technical Data
XLCR CAFÉ RACER (1977-1978)

Frame:	Double loop steel tube frame, steel tube swing arm, 2 shock absorbers
Fork:	Telescopic
Motor:	Air-cooled V2 Ironhead, OHV control, chain drive, 4-speed manual transmission
Cylinders:	2, 45° cylinder angle
Displacement:	60.81 cubic inches
Output:	approximately 61 hp
Construction Year:	1977-1978

FLT TOUR GLIDE (1980)
The Shovel as a Recreational Vehicle

Harley-Davidson's first super tourer was based on German and Japanese examples, such as the BMW 100 RT, Honda Gold Wing, and Yamaha XS 1100 Martini Special. In those years, the fairings by Craig Vetter sold like hotcakes.

Controversial appearance, but absolute touring suitability, that is the Tour Glide built from 1980 to 1983. The "80" in the motorcycle's designation stems from its displacement, which at 1340 cc was supposed to be sufficient to propel the bike, which in its production version weighed 778.8 pounds (354 kilograms).

The Late Shovel, which had been in production for two years, had proved to be a steady, powerful motor, which was especially important with this very heavy motorcycle.

Producing 65 hp, the Shovelhead motor propelled the Tour Glide to 95 miles per hour (153 kilometers per hour), which was very respectable for a bike of this size. Of course, with a price of $6,013, it was also Harley-Davidson's most expensive model. Nevertheless, 4,480 were built and sold to customers eager to ride long distances or used to comfort. The bike's equipment and prices surpassed the standard of a medium-size car on the Continent, but like so many other motorcycles from Milwaukee, it became a cult object.

To win over the touring clientele, the Motor Company designed a completely new bike, seeking and finding new paths in the process. First, the motor was equipped with a transistor ignition to improve ease of maintenance. As well, an enclosed chain box helped reduce oil spray from the drive chain. The FXB,

which also appeared in 1980, had a wear-resistant belt drive, which was to become a feature of Harley-Davidson bikes, but with the giant touring model they took no chances and stuck with the proven chain. The Tour Glide driver also enjoyed a five-speed transmission. Somewhat closer gear spacing did little to affect the motorcycle's performance, as the fifth gear was designed mainly as an overdrive, reducing revolutions and also fuel consumption. The Tour Glide's motor, not known for its smooth running, had rubber mounts. The three attachment points meant that almost no vibration reached the rider, significantly increasing comfort.

With bike speeds steadily rising, Harley-Davidson, of course, also worked on the brake system and equipped the FLT with two disc bakes on the front wheel and one on the back. The design of the Tour Glide's frame was equally courageous and even revolutionary. Despite weighing in excess of 880 pounds (400 kilograms) with a full tank and rider, the bike was supposed to be easy to maneuver and track perfectly straight. These are two things that, with a normal steering head, are usually changed by changing the angle of the steering head in this or that direction. As well, there were difficulties designing the new chassis, as the Tour

Left: The Electra Glide's top case offers plenty of room.

Right: Frame anchored for the first time—twin headlights for good road illumination.

Glide was supposed to remain stable whether driven one-up or two-up with full baggage. For this, Eric Buell was brought on board—and concentrated on the geometry of the new frame. He used a steel tube frame with swing arm and two shock struts. The Tour Glide's steering head had an extreme steering head angle of 65 degrees, something normally associated with a chopper. However, on the steering head, the forks were mounted with an offset and at an acute 62 degrees. As it turned out, this new method of chassis optimization was the correct decision.

The monstrous fairing added stiffness to the frame and there were no complaints about the driving behavior of the Tour Glide. At the same time, the fairing was a point on which opinions varied. Not only were its

dimensions enormous, but for many, the integrated twin headlights did not fit the classic Harley-Davidson image. The speedometer and tachometer were mounted directly on the handlebars, and the fairing had sufficient space for additional instruments and a radio with speakers, which caused some to ridicule the machine as a "musical steamboat."

Left: Twin discs up front. In the 80s, braking power still left something to be desired.

Right: Like sitting in a panoramic armchair— the passenger's seat.

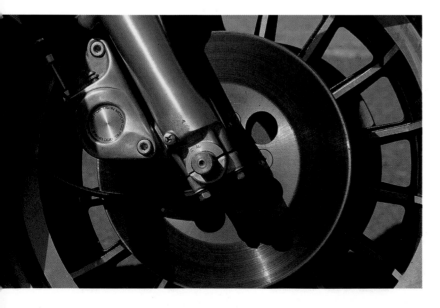

The instrument panel was more reminiscent of that of a road cruiser than a motorcycle.

The FLT Tour Glide was built until 1983. That year not only saw the end of production of the visually-controversial FLT model, but the end of the Shovelhead motor, which was replaced by the Evolution motor.

Below: Oil tank and seat—with the comfortable leather upholstery, it was possible to cover 600 miles per day.

Technical Data
FLT TOUR GLIDE (1980)

Frame:	Double loop steel tube frame, steel tube swing arm, 2 shock absorbers
Fork:	Telescopic
Motor:	Air-cooled V2 Shovelhead, OHV control, chain drive, 5-speed manual transmission
Cylinders:	2, 45° cylinder angle
Displacement:	80 cubic inches
Output:	approximately 64 hp
Construction Year:	1984-1994

FXE SUPER GLIDE (1982)
American Lifestyle on Two Wheels

The history of Harley-Davidson contains both spectacular milestones and no less spectacular flops. But there was also a model series that saved Harley-Davidson in the 1970s, and, at the same time, helped define the marque's image: the FX models.

The roots of the FX series lie in the late 1960s. The first sketches had already been drawn—by none other than chief designer Willie G. Davidson—when Harley-Davidson was taken over by AMF in 1969. He had recognized the signs of the times early on and developed a motorcycle that was to be a base for "customizing" by the customer, and he also envisaged a large number of factory-built model variants. The first FX Super Glide of 1971 was still a mixture of cruiser and sport bike, for the oversized boat tail disturbed the harmony of the overall picture somewhat. Many FX buyers simply removed the bulky rear end and replaced it with a chopper bench seat. In the second model year the motorcycle was given a more pleasing seat, and the success story had its start. Production began with 4,700 units in 1971, but in the following years the figures rose rapidly to 6,500, 7,625, and 9,233 (FX and FXE). Only more Sportsters were leaving the production line, which was now in York, Pennsylvania.

Chopper style for the Harley fan: the 1982 Super Glide.

From today's viewpoint, the FX can be seen as the first production cruiser bike: low seat position, raised bars, and forward-positioned foot pegs summon the "Easy Rider" feeling, contrasting with the high-tech sport bikes coming from Japan and Europe. Seated on the wide saddle, hands on the buckeye handlebars, the rider can enjoy the full song of the V-Twins—the theoretical maximum speed of 102 miles per hour (165 kilometers per hour) remains theoretical. The braking system from the AMF days also makes an overly aggressive riding style inadvisable. The FX buyer of the 1970s did so out of passion—in the Eighties because he wanted the original: A wave of soft choppers from Japan had been patterned after the FX, creating additional interest in the V-Twins from Milwaukee. The derivatives of the FX model series caused a stir: The Fat Bob, Wide Glide, and Low Rider were all unique designs, but shared a common chassis and running gear. Since 1978, the Shovelhead motor of 1966 has been bored out to 1,200 and 1,340 cc, which at least gave Harley-Davidson an advantage in displacement over the copies from the Far East.

In 1980, the company released a special model, the FXB Sturgis, which was to be a trail blazer for the model history of Harley-Davidson: Built to mark the fortieth anniversary of the motorcycle rally in the Black Hills of South Dakota, it was the first production motorcycle to have belt drive as primary and end drive. What then was still regarded with distrust, can now hardly be imagined as anything else. As they are today, the quiet, easy-to-maintain belts were made by Gates, and the three years the FXB (the "B" stood for Belt Drive) was in production provided valuable data about the service life of the belt drive, which now is installed in every Harley-Davidson motorcycle. Ten

years after the unveiling of the Super Glide, Harley-Davidson decided to step away from AMF. Under the leadership of Vaughan Beals and Willie G. Davidson, the announcement of 26 February 1981 became fact on the 16th of June: "The eagle soars alone" was the new motto. By then, of course, the 1982 model year had been completely developed: The conversion of the production lines in York to the next model year began in July, the 1982 model year began in August 1981. All of that year's FX Super Glides were therefore true Harleys.

In fact, the 1982 model year did not look much different from the 1971 one: The XL, FL, and FX basic models were only divided into a larger number of sub-models. There was also the "birthday model" of the Sportster, which was celebrating its twenty-fifth.

The final phase of the Shovelhead: typical Harley-Davidson equipment with "cowbell" horn and chromed ignition coil cover.

The Shovelhead motor of 1982: a technological dinosaur in the age of high-tech bikes.

The 1982 model year brought the FX series to the latest level of technology: Offered were the FXE Super Glide, FXS Low Rider, FXWG Wide Glide, FXB Sturgis, and two new models which, with a completely new frame with rubber motor mounts, was to level the future for the entire series. The FXR and FXRS Super Glide II were the FX models designed for the Evolution motor, then still under development. Today, even halfway original Harley-Davidsons from this period are almost impossible to find, for most bikes fell victim to customization and were cannibalized. The reverse side of the coin: Replacement parts for these bikes are relatively easy to find—one just has to keep one's eyes open at swap meets.

Left and right: Fork tubes and braces are filigree.

The cockpit: neutral and oil indicator lights mounted in the headlight.

Below: Chopper feeling with wide handlebars.

Technical Data
FXE SUPER GLIDE (1982)

Frame:	Double loop steel tube frame, steel tube swing arm, 2 shock absorbers
Fork:	Telescopic fork
Motor:	Air-cooled V2 Shovelhead, OHV control, chain drive, 5-speed manual transmission
Cylinders:	2, 45° cylinder angle
Displacement:	80 cubic inches
Output:	approximately 65 hp
Construction Year:	1971-1982

XR 1000 (1983)
The Racer for the Street

No matter what today's marketing strategies claim, the XR 1000 was simply "racing pure" and of all Harleys was closest to the racetrack.

L oud, powerful, and nasty is certainly the best way to describe the Harley-Davidson XR 1000. It was a true racer from the house of Harley-Davidson which struck fear into the hearts of competitors on country roads and was the fastest production Harley to date. With a healthy portion of courage, riding skill and the proverbial knife between the teeth, the XR 1000 could be leaned over and pounded around corners in a fashion usually reserved for sport bikes. A generous portion of torque and adequate performance made the motorcycle a popular race bike for private riders. In an effort to stimulate sales, the XR 1000 was unveiled at the Daytona Bike Week, where the Battle of the Twins also took part.

Jay Springsteen won the legendary race at the first go, but in 1983, the shocking purchase price of just under $7,000 scared off many buyers, especially since the price of a "normal" Sportster was only about $4,000.

One year before the unveiling of the XR 1000, the Sportster had undergone a serious makeover for its twenty-fifth birthday with revised frame, running gear, and motor. The XR 1000 was thus the gem of the model range, but

with a price to match. Nevertheless, about 1,500 of the road racers were sold and the prices continued to rise, for the number of bikes that survived the race track or succumbed to amateur mechanics is very small.

Visually, this predecessor of all naked bikes was easy to distinguish from the normal models. New cylinder heads, red stripes on the hubs, raised twin pipes, and two carburetors on the right side were just several of the racer's features. The XR 1000 was even given a separate cover for the ignition cap. The centerpiece of the XR 1000 was of course the motor. The 1,000 cc motor was based on the existing Sportster motor but had been thoroughly modified.

The renowned Jerry Branch developed new aluminum cylinder heads for the XR 1000 and these

provided better fuel flow and were attached to the motor block by threaded studs. With the special pistons, the motor had a compression ratio of 9:1 and lighter connecting rods, a prerequisite for a light, high-revving motor. Two unmistakable 1.4 -inch (36-mm) Dell'Orto carburetors with accelerator pumps were positioned on the right side. Equally imposing were the exhaust pipes, arranged dirt track style, which in addition to identifying the model year made the bike sound like a Harley should. The production version produced a solid 70 hp, but for many, that was not enough. There was a tuning kit for the 484-pound (220-kilogram) motorcycle designed to exploit the 1,000 cc motor's reserves. While the so-called 100 hp kit only resulted in an output of 90 hp, the XR

Power pack: Despite the traditional 45° cylinder angle, the XR motor was a very compact design— and was unable to hide its derivation from the Sportster power plant.

Left: Small but fine! With the XR tank one rode from gas station to gas station and got to know new people...

Right: Each cylinder had its own carburetor.

1000's impressive torque made it almost unbeatable among V-twins. A special camshaft, pistons which raised the compression ratio to 10:1, and a special racing exhaust system provided the additional performance.

Of course, in addition to being fast, the motorcycle had to handle well and have good brakes. And so, instead of the usual spoked wheels, Harley-Davidson used the newly-developed cast hubs and gave the XR 1000 two generously dimensioned disc brakes on the front wheel. With a four-speed transmission, the production bike was able to reach 115 miles per hour (185 kilometers per hour), which today might not seem like much; but for a naked bike from the early Eighties, it was an amazing

achievement. The XR 1000 was delivered with tires that one might describe as adventurous. A Dunlop 100/90 R19 up front and a 130/90 R16 in the rear did not exactly make the XR 1000 appear to be a bike that was over-tired, and those who raced with them earned heightened respect. The XR 1000 was only in the company catalogue for two years. It had originally been conceived as a limited edition of 1,100 motorcycles, which was expected to cover the demand for dedicated racing machines. In 1984, the model's second and last production year, the XR 1000 could also be had in Harley-Davidson racing colors, black and orange. The only examples still in that original finish are to be found in museums and the hands of private collectors.

Left: Not really needed on the XR—rearview mirror...

Right: Small headlight, tachometer and speedometer.

From dirt track to
the street: No other
Harley had ever been
so uncompromisingly
trimmed for
performance.

Below: Simple and
easy to overlook—the
instrument cluster.

Technical Data
XR 1000 (1983-1984)

Frame:	Double loop steel tube frame, steel tube swing arm, 2 shock absorbers
Fork:	Telescopic fork
Motor:	Air-cooled V2 XR, OHV control, chain drive, 4-speed manual transmission
Cylinders:	2, 45° cylinder angle
Displacement:	30.17 cubic inches
Output:	approximately 70 hp
Construction Year:	1983-1984

FXRT SPORT GLIDE (1984)
Harley-Davidson's Rolling Secret

An expedient with style: The FXRT Sport Glide used the fairing of an entirely different Harley-Davidson model.

There have been many attempts by Harley-Davidson to produce a sport touring model to complement the Electra Glide monster tourer. None of these experiments had such an interesting history as the FXRT, and the truth behind the "RT" story is almost completely unknown. Even many Harley insiders remain oblivious to this part of the company's history—for apart from a single press release by a former Harley public relations officer, the public, for whom it had been designed, never saw the bike. We are talking about Harley-Davidson's first liquid-cooled superbike, developed in cooperation with Porsche like the later V-Rod, and powered by a motor that could not have

been more atypical for a Harley. It was a highly-modern V4 with overhead camshafts and numerous technical details that were ahead of their time. The project was dubbed "Nova."

Anyone who closely examines the FXRT will subliminally guess that this or that part was not designed for this motorcycle. Neither the large integrated signal lights nor the general lines match the shape of the tank, and the inner fairing and mounts seemed to have been cobbled together as an afterthought. And why does a fairing have cooling inlets that go nowhere? The official history of Harley-Davidson

written by David K. Wright states: "Mounted rigidly on the frame, the FXRT's fairing was shaped by HD engineers in a wind tunnel and was designed for maximum top speed and fuel consumption." This is close to the truth—but for a different motorcycle.

Developed at the end of the AMF period—and thus paid for by AMF—the Nova motors had displacements of 800 and 1000 cc and were similar in appearance and performance to the VFR power plants by Honda. As Harley-Davidson was later to discover with the V-Rod models, it was difficult to provide an exclusively liquid-cooled motor with sufficient cooling without the radiator taking up too much space. The Harley-Davidson engineers stumbled upon an extremely inventive solution: The touring model had a fairing through which cooling air—via the previously mentioned air inlets, which look so out of place on the FXRT—was directed through channels on the motor to the rear-mounted radiator. Additional fans in the rear further aided cooling.

Though a technically convincing solution, the "Nova" was a flop at a dealer presentation: That's supposed to be a Harley? Unthinkable. In the turbulent times of the buy-back, it was easy for the new management to let the project drop—the prototypes made their way to a corner of the secret museum, where they sat ignored for many years. And everyone who saw the Nova agreed: The bike was ugly.

The development work had not been for nothing, however, and some of the production tools were used for various production parts. A new use was also sought for the fairing and the FX models seemed the ideal candidate. At the peak of its popularity and in the midst of the conversion to the Evolution motor in 1984, the Nova's fairing was

placed on the FXR together with the FLT's air filter box and new saddlebags. Harley took from the designation of the BMW R 100 RT and the new tourer was complete. At a time when Craig Vetter was selling his fairings like slices of bread, and touring bikes by BMW, Honda, and Yamaha were top sellers, the FXRT was just another tourer in the Harley-Davidson program. No one was astonished that Harley suddenly had three concurrent touring machines, the Electra Glide, the Tour Glide, and the Sport Glide, in its program. At the same

The new motor: The new power plant was called the Evolution motor and was to propel Harley-Davidson to new heights.

Whether with just saddlebags or the additional top case for touring, with the Sport Glide, one could get from one place to another quickly.

time, the fairing was supposed to be used on another model that would soon be spread across the USA: the FXRP. The long production life of the "emergency solution" was in part due to the use of the broad fairing for police motorcycles, which were used by many highway patrol units.

When production began, there were overlaps that made several Harley-Davidson models real collectors' items. A small number of the first FXRT models made in 1984 were still equipped with the 80-cubic-inch Shovelhead motor—the literature

contains numerous illustrations of the FXRT firstborns. The majority of the bikes, however, were given the brand new Evolution motor, which remained in use until production ended in 1992. With a comfortable touring seat with sissy bar, saddlebags from GFK, and mid-mounted foot rests—the passenger's pegs were also fixed—the FXRT was a really practical sport tourer. In fact, the first FXRT was no more than an FXR with the "Nova" fairing bolted on, with paint and pinstripes to blend it in.

Where did they go? The cooling inlets had disappeared from the fairing, for good reason.

Below: A touring seat. Wide leather saddle for many miles of riding enjoyment.

Technical Data
FXRT SPORT GLIDE (1984)

Frame:	Double loop steel tube frame, steel tube swing arm, 2 shock absorbers
Fork:	Telescopic
Motor:	Air-cooled V2, OHV control, belt drive, battery 5-speed manual transmission
Cylinders:	2, 45° cylinder angle
Displacement:	80 cubic inches
Output:	approximately 61 hp
Construction Year:	1984-1992

FLTC TOUR GLIDE ULTRA CLASSIC (1989)
Pure American Lifestyle

Long-distance traveling is in the blood of Americans: Distances in America are truly "continental," and between the fantastic landscapes that are everywhere on the continent, there are often thousands of miles of lonesome wilderness, endless cornfields, and absolutely straight interstates, with at best an occasional rest stop to provide a little relief. From the beginning, the ability to bridge these distances was decisive in the development of the American motorcycle. Large-displacement motors promised performance at low rpm and minimal engine wear. Even the first Harley single-cylinder machines had to prove themselves in endurance runs:

In 1907, Walter Davidson rode the Silent Grey Fellow in the top three of the Chicago–Kokomo endurance run, a distance of 414 miles.

Harley-Davidson itself promoted motorcycle tourism in the company magazine, *Enthusiast*. Touring and trip reports from all over the world filled many of the magazine's pages. Leafing through the old booklets, one can only tip his hat to the descriptions of tours and trips to exotic lands, some of which are closed to us today and some still as difficult to reach as they were in the 20s and 30s. Until the arrival of the KH and Sportster models, all Harley-Davidson

Harley's touring bike: The Tour Glide promised pure touring comfort for the driver and passenger.

Running boards for secure footing. The weather protection provided by the leg guards is rather meager.

motorcycles were geared towards touring, and so it remained with the big twins until into the 1970s.

Introduced in 1965, the Electra Glide became emblematic of the American touring dinosaur—and can still be found in a wide variety of variations in the models offered. The Electra Glide's failure to find favor in the European market is due to the different mentality of the motorcyclists there and belies the importance of the motorcycle in the Harley program. In the United States, the E-Glide is still a long runner and is not only sold, but ridden.

At the end of the 1970s, new touring motorcycles challenged the Electra Glide for the title of Queen of the Highways. The Honda Gold Wing, Kawasaki Z 1300, Yamaha XS 1100, and the BMW R 100 RT provided stiff competition, in some cases offering luxury equipment and accessories from cola can holders to CB radios, but mainly engine performance and reliability. Harley saw its faithful

customers switching to other brands—an alarming sign.

The conversion of the Electra Glide into a luxury tourer went hand in hand with the development of a new model, designed primarily to respond to Honda's attack: the FLT Tour Glide. What at first glance looked like a modified Electra Glide was in fact a completely unique motorcycle. In contrast to the E-Glide's handlebar fairing that turned with the forks, the Tour Glide's fairing was attached rigidly to the frame. The steering geometry was more reminiscent of a sport bike than a cruiser: Once a rider got used to the fairing, and the restricted view of the road, he found that the Tour Glide negotiated sharp corners surprisingly easily.

While the first models were still equipped with the 80-cubic-inch Shovelhead motor, it later used the Evolution and Twin-Cam motors as these came along. In the case of the Twin Cam, it introduced the new motor

The large muffler,
production version.

a year ahead of the popular Softail models. The reason: As Harley could never match the vibration-free qualities of the Honda horizontally opposed four-cylinder motors, it instead mounted the entire block of motor, primary drive, and transmission in rubber blocks, following the example set by Norton in the 1970s. This reduced the amount of vibration reaching the rider without hampering the typical "beat" of the V-Twin. In 1988, Honda introduced a six-cylinder motor with a displacement of 1500 cc—Harley couldn't put up with that. For the 1989 model year, the Ultra Classic versions of the Electra and Tour Glide appeared, offering deluxe paint and luxury equipment with cruise control, elaborate 80-watt stereo system, radio, CB radio, speakers fore and aft, and stowage space in the fairing.

Although only 603 examples of the luxury tourer were ordered, including fifteen with sidecar, the Tour Glide remained a popular machine among long-distance riders, especially after the introduction of the twin-cam motors. The special "Screamin' Eagle" models produced by Harley's CVO customizing department, which each year created exciting special models, sold out several years in a row, even before they reached their final customers. Harley dealers had reserved the collectors' items for themselves.

Left: The tank holds
sufficient fuel for
more than 150 miles
(250 kilometers).

Right: Generous seat
area for the driver.

The frame-anchored fairing offered room for a radio, cassette player, and CB radio.

Center: Chrome baroque—ornamental guard on the front fender.

Below: Television chair comfort for the passenger and still room for the sleeping bags.

Technical Data

FLTC TOUR GLIDE ULTRA CLASSIC (1989)

Frame:	Double loop steel tube frame, steel tube swing arm, 2 shock absorbers
Fork:	Telescopic fork
Motor:	Air-cooled V2 Evolution, OHV control, belt drive, 5-speed manual transmission
Cylinders:	2, 45° cylinder angle
Displacement:	80 cubic inches
Output:	approximately 64 hp
Construction Year:	1984-1994

FXDWG DYNA WIDE GLIDE (1993)
90 Years and Not Even a Little Quiet

When the first Wide Glide appeared in 1980, the general reaction was "Wow." Many factory choppers had been made in Milwaukee during the Seventies, but the first Wide Glide to leave the production line looked like a true custom bike: black-finished engine and transmission case, the edges of the cylinders and heads polished, and the body parts finished in a special black paint with yellow and red flames. That was the stuff of which Harley-Davidson dreams were made. As the marketing department had calculated, from the beginning the Wide Glide was the sales hit of the year—and the most produced machine in the 1980 model year. Examples numbering 6,085 rolled off the production lines in York,

Pennsylvania, beginning the Wide Glide's triumphal march. The custom paint for the first time answered the customers' requests for individualized models—the Wide Glide was the center of attention at every motorcycle meet and in front of every ice cream parlor. As a direct offshoot of the FX series, the machine also possessed excellent handling characteristics. The 80-cubic-inch motor—the Shovelhead in the first two years, then the Evo and Twin Cam—ensured adequate propulsion.

The custom appearance of the Wide Glide was enhanced by the contrast of its 16-inch rear wheel and narrow 21-inch front wheel. Not quite as extreme

Easy Rider in a Sunday suit: Dyna Wide Glide with ninetieth Anniversary paint.

as the wild custom bike conversions at the shows in Daytona Beach and Sturgis, but nevertheless with a clear message: Here I am! In fact, the first Wide Glide was a ready-made outlaw bike—although Harley never specially courted that customer group. In fact, many motorcycle clubs drove, and drive, FX series bikes and value them for their robust performance. The model has undergone constant development and remains in the Harley-Davidson program, although with a different character: In 1993 "the wild one" was turned into a domesticated anniversary issue—what one can do with colors! The FXDWG earned its extra letter as a result of the adoption of the Dyna Frame. Wide front fork, one-piece Fat Bob tank, and the exhaust system were coordinated with the bike's styling, but somehow the steam had gone out of the visual appearance. Fine custom, not the outlaw look, was now hip, the rebel was dressed in a confirmation outfit, for grandmother was celebrating her birthday.

While some small companies survive to reach at least their fiftieth birthday, Harley-Davidson, as one of the few motorcycle manufacturers with an unbroken production tradition, had survived several economic crises, sales of the company and two world wars. An advertisement in the German press declared: "Recessions, stock market crash, depressions, 17 American presidents, fashion trends and a Marlon Brando film … We survived it all." That Marlon Brando had ridden a Triumph in his movie *The Wild One*, while the outlaw Lee Marvin was placed on a Harley, had obviously left behind wounds. And in 1990, Harley-Davidson was on the verge of an unbelievable success story which was to make the motorcycle maker from Milwaukee one of the most familiar brand names in the world.

The 1990 Dyna Wide Glide offered typical chopper features such as a forward foot rest system, low-seat position and rearwards-curving handlebars: In 1980, the Buckhorn

Birthday everywhere: even on the sissy bar.

handlebars had given way to monkey bars, which were frowned on by the police in a number of states. In Florida, monkey bars higher than the rider's shoulders could result in a ticket.

The Bobber style rear fender, dubbed "Bobtail" by Harley, offered excellent protection against road dirt and a small sissy bar contributed to passenger comfort. The 1993 special model had plenty of chrome and a special finish of anthracite gray and silver with a red cheat line. The tank emblem consisted of the number 90 between two eagle wings.

The company's anniversary was celebrated in June 1993—in what was the biggest party Milwaukee had ever seen—and was a small foretaste of what lay ahead on the 95th and 100th anniversaries. Also celebrated was the tenth birthday of the Harley Owner Group, or HOG, a quasi company motorcycle club, which made

A piece of American freedom celebrates its ninetieth birthday.

Milwaukee a city under motorcycle siege. On 12 June 1993, Willie G. Davidson led a group of 15,000 motorcycle riders from Kenosha to the Milwaukee fairgrounds. And, for the first time, the highways were closed just for Harley-Davidson riders, when a convoy of 100,000 Harley-Davidson motorcycles headed for Milwaukee. And the real boom time for the company was yet to come, in the next decade.

Technical Data
FXDWG DYNA WIDE GLIDE (1993) (90TH ANNIVERSARY)

Frame:	Double loop steel tube frame, steel tube swing arm, 2 shock absorbers
Fork:	Telescopic fork
Motor:	Air-cooled V2 Evolution, OHV control, chain drive, battery coil ignition, 5-speed manual transmission
Cylinders:	2, 45° cylinder angle
Displacement:	80 cubic inches
Output:	approximately 48 hp
Construction Year:	1993

FLSTC HERITAGE SOFTAIL (1997)
The Harley for Everyone

Much too pretty to be mean: The Heritage Softail plays with the Harley-Davidson designs of earlier years.

The Heritage Softail is probably the bike that most Harley riders and fans consider to be the true Harley-Davidson. The best way to describe the model is big, comfortable, and with a hint of nostalgia. Outwardly, the bike resembles the Duo Glide in many respects—the large two-piece tank, the dashboard, the spoked wheels and much more. The big difference is that the Duo Glide still has two normal shock struts and a simple swing arm. The Softail models appear to have a rigid rear frame, but in fact there are two shock absorbers concealed beneath the frame. The swing arm design invented by American Bill Davis was adopted by Harley-Davidson and the company purchased the patent, which would prove to be a clever move. The Heritage Softail, production of which began in 1987, embodied the Harley community's new way of life. With the Evo motor, whose 527.6 inches (1,340 centimeters) produces 65 hp, the Heritage Softail has a reliable power plant suitable for everyday use which enables the bike to reach 102 miles per hour (165 kilometers per hour).

Of course, like all Harley-Davidson models, the motorcycle has a maintenance-free belt drive and an easy-to-shift five-speed transmission. The steel tube frame offered sufficient stability and was very torsion resistant. The single-piston brakes, however, were often criticized; however, that was also later changed by Harley-Davidson. The tires of the Heritage Softail were still quite narrow in keeping with the classic look of the Heritage, whose most noticeable feature was its 130 x 16 front tire. Other features of the Heritage were the big front and rear fenders, reminiscent of the Duo Glide, but also its spoked wheels, which needed plenty of care to keep the spokes shiny.

The versions and special models of the Heritage Softail are seemingly endless. Over the years, the bike has been sold with a large touring windshield, saddle bags, and sissy bar, and various styles of handlebar. One of the most eye-catching models was surely the black and white special model with a cowhide seat. Also very popular is the classic version with the rivet-lined seat and the tassels on the seat and saddlebag.

In 1990, Harley-Davidson presented a derivative of the Heritage: the so-called Fat Boy with silver paint overall and disc wheels. For some, the motorcycle designed by Willy G. was

Clearly arranged: The central ignition switch and large speedometer promise order.

Fine finish characterizes the Harley-Davidsons of the new generation. The tank still consists of two halves.

a break with style; for others, it was a return to the company's aggressive, yet sporty, image. Much to the horror of the customer, the bike was already a true custom bike with no trim or accessories to take away from the pure look of the bike. In 1997, the Heritage Springer with springer forks was added to the line, completing the nostalgic look of the motorcycle. Most models continued to be sold with conventional forks, however, on account of their excellent driving qualities and level of comfort. In 1997, the Company's FL series was, of course, also sold with telescopic forks and various two-color paint schemes. The wide front tire and additional headlight completed the picture. The riveted saddle bags and the seat, with the passenger seated on a raised pedestal, were also characteristics of the model range.

Many owners used accessories to complete the classic look. A bewildering variety of accessories is available, and consequently, many Heritage Softail models are one-of-a-kind motorcycles. Whether it is mirrors, which is where customizing often begins, chrome cover with golden eagle and "Live to Ride" legend, or different seats and instruments—almost anything is possible. The fishtail exhausts are, of course, very popular, combining the classic look with a not always quite legal sound. Even home tuning kits, the so-called "Screaming Eagle" products, are available for the Heritage. Many motorcycles have been modified with different camshafts, air filters, carburetors and ignition boxes, increasing power to almost 90 hp. The Heritage Softail is an absolutely

comfortable motorcycle for two persons, which because of its decent braking power should be ridden with a degree of respect and foresight.

Technical Data
FLSTC HERITAGE SOFTAIL (1997)

Frame:	Double loop steel tube frame, Softail steel tube swing arm, 2 shock absorbers under the frame
Fork:	Telescopic fork
Motor:	Air-cooled V2 Evolution, OHV control, belt drive, 5-speed manual transmission
Cylinders:	2, 45° cylinder angle
Displacement:	80 cubic inches
Output:	approximately 56 hp
Construction Year:	1997

FXSTB NIGHT TRAIN (1998)
Black is Beautiful!

The 1998 model year was marked by the celebration of the ninety-fifth anniversary of the Harley-Davidson company, which took place in Milwaukee in September of the year. Several hundred thousand Harley-Davidson owners celebrated the anniversary and numerous production models were offered in an unusual brown and beige anniversary paint scheme. It may seem surprising that Harley-Davidson chose this particular time to introduce a motorcycle painted in simple black only: the "Night Train." As one of the lowest-priced Softail models, the FXSTB, as the official designation went, quickly became a best seller and remains so to this day.

At that time, Harley-Davidson was enjoying unparalleled success. Since the start of the 1990s, sales figures had been on a steady upswing, and the sale of accessories and clothing poured money into the company's coffers. The building block system, the result of years of experience, made it possible to develop a new model by exchanging individual components such as forks, seat, tank, and fenders. Within a few years, the Softail series was divided into numerous sub-models. Each of these was aimed at a type of rider and yet differed from the other models so significantly that each

Black in black: The Night Train is not just made for bad boys.

Black crinkle paint not only makes the engine dark optically—it improves heat dissipation considerably.

had its own character. Individuality was a major priority, both for the marque and its customers.

No motorcycle better illustrated Harley-Davidson's close attention to market trends than the Night Train. In the 1990s, many hard-core bikers rode black bikes—in Europe and the USA. Freely adapted from Henry Ford's motto, "You can have your auto in any color, so long as it's black," the "bad bikes" dominated the motorcycle magazines and the bike shows. Restricted to the color black,

Clearly arranged control elements: Drag bars require the rider to adopt a forward-leaning seat position—or very long arms.

supplemented by selected chrome parts, the bike was aimed as this customer group, as well as at the "spare time bad boy," the stockbroker or dentist who in his free time donned his leather jacket and rode his Harley toward the sunset and away from his mid-life crisis. There was no better machine for this than the Night Train: Harley feeling pure and without compromise.

First introduced in 1984, the Softail or FXST series sprung from the FXWG Wide Glide and represented Harley's ultimate design: The combination of modern spring comfort with the look of an old rigid frame accounted for the fascination with the Harley-Davidson Softail models, which played a major role in the company's success in the 1990s. The shock struts were placed beneath the transmission in the center of the twin-tube frame—and were thus invisible to the observer.

The 1998 Night Train was the logical continuation of the series: The 80-cubic-inch Evolution motor delivered a bubbling 56 hp to the rear wheel via a fully-developed primary drive and belt drive, by then standard on all Harley-Davidson motorcycles. Weighing 644.6 pounds (293 kilograms), the Night Train lived up to its name. Compared to other contemporary motorcycles, the power-to-weight ration was similar to that of a locomotive—but that had never bothered Harley fans. While the Softail models were usually at the upper end of the Harley price scale, the Night Train's price was kept to an absolute minimum, allowing first-time buyers to have a Softail big twin which they could later customize from the accessory catalogue at the Harley dealer. Since it first hit the market, countless customers worldwide have used it as a base for custom conversions, installed wide-tire kits

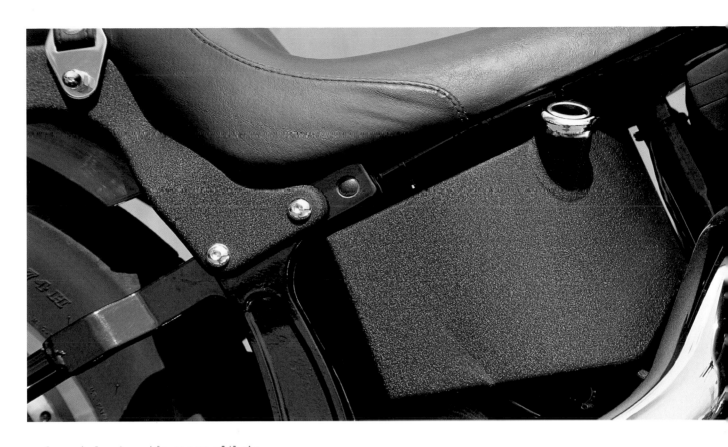

and carried out a wide range of their own modifications. Not surprisingly, it is difficult to find a Night Train in its original configuration. The motor, transmission case, primary drive, oil tank and fender struts are covered with crinkle black paint, while the tank, fenders and tail are painted gloss black. With straight handlebars, forward foot rests, and seat designed more for solo riding than two-up, the Night Train also fully conveys the "outlaw bike" image to the rider: get on, give it the gas, pull away! Suddenly, a production Harley looks like the bikes ridden by the bad boys twenty years earlier. That's some kind of evolution.

Dark, but cool: paint like a stealth fighter.

Technical Data
FXSTB NIGHT TRAIN (1998)

Frame:	Double loop steel tube frame, Softail steel tube swing arm, 2 shock absorbers under the frame
Fork:	Telescopic fork
Motor:	Air-cooled V2 Evolution, OHV control, belt drive, 5-speed manual transmission
Cylinders:	2, 45° cylinder angle
Displacement:	80 cubic inches
Output:	approximately 65 hp
Construction Year:	1998

FLSTF FAT BOY (1998)
Fat Salute to the 95th Birthday

A Fat Boy with spoked wheels? There really is such a thing. When established in 1998, the company's "Custom Vehicle Organization" (CVO) introduced three converted Fat Boys, which were photographed exclusively by Dieter Rebmann. Whether these machines ever left the factory is not known.

The Fat Boy is absolutely the Harley-Davidson macho bike. The Fat Boy is linked with the marque's success in the 1990s like almost no other machine. Like so many successful models, the Fat Boy was conceived on the sketchbook of chief designer Willie G. Davidson, who was able to draw on Harley-Davidson's extensive design history for this model. The massive forks with faired tubes was reminiscent of the 1949 Hydra Glide, which was the first Harley-Davidson to use telescopic forks. A massive headlight sits on the metal fairing and is just as much a feature of the Fat Boy as the massive 16-inch disc wheels. Disc wheels, which were supposed to protect the spokes against dirt, or—in the case of military machines—were easier to clean, have come into vogue now and then during the history of motorcycles. In the 1990s, when streamlined aerodynamic designs and lightweight sports wheels were popular, such a wheel was an anachronism. But it was one that was intentionally chosen by Willie G. The overall optics of the Fat Boy were so opposed to conventional styling that there were only two options for the machine: top or flop.

For the 1990 model year, the Fat Boy was presented to an astounded

The 1998 motor had the anniversary badge of the company's 95th jubilee.

public: the massive appearance of the Fat Boy was underlined by its finish, for on this bike everything was "Heavy Metal." Fenders, tank, and oil tank were all pressed from thick sheet metal—and the accessories, too, were cut from solid metal. At the beginning of the 1990s, Harley-Davidson had a good feeling for what the customer wanted. And so a bike weighing 660 pounds (300 kilograms) was acceptable. Otherwise, the Fat Boy made use of the building block system, which Harley had been using successfully for a long time. The Fat Boy was derived from the Softail Custom and Heritage Softail models. Introduced in 1984, the Softail frame combined the appearance of a rigid frame with spring comfort that made it suitable for day-to-day use. The spring travel of the shock absorber located under the motor is still rather modest— for on this bike, look is more important than riding characteristics. This is also underlined by the paint work, which, for the first time, is a complete work

of art that includes the frame: while all production frames are black when they leave the paint shop, in this case, Fine Silver Metallic was also used on the framework. Apart from chrome, aluminum, stainless steel, and silver paint, the only colored accents are the yellow stripes on the rocker boxes. In later years, these were adapted to match the basic color of the machine.

The idea of the Fat Boy came at just the right time, for the macho machine made its next big appearance on movie screens the following year: in *Terminator 2*. No matter how many times it is seen on video or television, the scene in which Arnold Schwarzenegger "borrows" his outfit in a biker bar is still cool—provided you are not the owner of the Fat Boy. Even though the motorcycle is given just a brief role by director James Cameron, no moviegoer will ever forget the breathtaking stunt with the jump off the bridge into the drainage canals of Los Angeles.

Left: Few custom bikes could have created a sensation for the CVO than a Fat Boy with spoked wheels. Mission accomplished...

Right: Chrome fittings and everything that is expensive: The CVO motorcycles are known for having plenty of accessories installed.

An impressive 4,400 machines were produced the first year and they were literally torn from the hands of the dealers—it was the beginning of a success story. When the decade ended, the Fat Boy had outsold every other Harley-Davidson model—not bad for a machine that was met with ridicule by the motorcycle press and whose disc wheels were eyed mistrustfully on account of their side-wind sensitivity. The fact that the Fat Boy rarely entered the speed range where side-wind was a factor, is another story altogether.

The year 1998 was the time of another big company anniversary and Harley-Davidson celebrated its 95th birthday—not just in Milwaukee, but worldwide. Faaker Lake in Carinthia witnessed the first outbreak of "Harleymania" in Europe, and even Willie G. Davidson crossed the big pond to visit and led a parade of several thousand Harley riders on a thirty-seven mile (sixty-kilometer) excursion around Wörther Lake. Anyone who wanted to take part in the parade on a 1998 Fat Boy in the anniversary paint scheme would had to have ordered his machine months ahead of time. By then, demand had exceeded supply and Harley-Davidson dealers all over the world were experiencing their golden age. The "95 Years" emblem stood out against the modest medium gray finish. Its place in the Harley-Davidson program is as solid as the machine's appearance—and if there is a scarcity of Fat Boys in original condition from any production year, each year one can order a brand-new, original classic. Even with minor modifications, as with good action films, one can be certain that there will be progress. Or as the Terminator says: "I'll be back!"

Even the running boards—expensive accessories instead of standard production.

Control of the road? From the rider's point of view, the machine is pure Fat Boy.

Below: Stitched into the seat— 95 Years logo.

Technical Data
FLSTF FAT BOY (1998)
(95TH ANNIVERSARY CVO SPECIAL)

Frame:	Double loop steel tube frame, Softail steel tube swing arm, 2 shock absorbers under the frame
Fork:	Telescopic fork
Motor:	Air-cooled V2 Evolution, OHV control, belt drive, 5-speed transmission
Cylinders:	2, 45° cylinder angle
Displacement:	80 cubic inches
Output:	approximately 65 hp
Construction Year:	1998

VRSCA V-ROD (2001)
Harley-Davidson and Porsche— Revolution from Milwaukee and Zuffenhausen

Not only is the VRSCA aimed at an entirely new group of customers, it is also the first Harley-Davidson motorcycle with liquid cooling. In 2001, this split the entire Harley community into two camps, one which welcomed progress, and one which declared that this was not "a true Harley." Whatever the case, progress through the Revolution motor could no longer be stopped, and the Porsche-developed motor catapulted the V-Rod into, for Harley-Davidson, uncharted rpm and speed ranges. The term Power Cruiser was born. Both the motor and frame were new developments, with greater torsional stiffness and riding stability than any previous Harley.

American design meets German technology: The V-Rod was the motorcycle that dominated magazine cover pages in 2001 and 2002!

The first kilometers covered in Europe were in Faak, Austria, where the VRSCA was unveiled in 2001. After their meeting in Salzburg, the directors from the USA didn't want to miss the opportunity to personally drive the bikes over the Austrian roads to Faaker Lake. These gentlemen were still not quite real bikers. After the motorcycles were cleaned following their rain tour, they were revealed to the public, who could look at and sat on the bikes. This, of course, wasn't enough for everyone. Everyone wanted more—a proper road test.

When the interview with Jeff Bleustein was over, the journalists

rushed to the next date with Bernd Gneithing of Harley Germany, who promised a ride on the V-Rod. The information from the highest level: "I'll call you if the weather is good." Wow, that was a word! Anticipation mixed with hope for sun and dry roads. Then the desired call: "Come in an hour, the bike is ready." The keys were handed over and the first driving tests on European soil began.

After the just 984-foot-long (300 meters) stretch out of the Harley village took a full ten minutes, there was no longer any doubt: This was a real looker. Finally, the tank beneath the seat was filled, the seat folded down, and off we went. Despite its long wheelbase of 67.4 inches (1,713 mms), the bike's handling soon became apparent, for never did I have to avoid so many people who tried to stop me to have a look at the bike. After we

had left the masses of fans behind us, it was time. Turn, turn, and turn some more. The throttle was handled cautiously in the first turns, but after a few kilometers I began to feel at one with the bike and the test program could begin. The ground clearance was an invitation to drive up a pass and on the way back test the brakes. On the uphill climb, even a few sport bikes were no more than rolling obstacles, thanks to a completely new, torsionally-stiff frame design and the generously-sized aluminum swing arm. That, combined with low cross section tires with dimensions of 120/70 ZR 19 up front and 180/55 ZR 18 in the back, plus the stable 1.9-inch fork (49-mm), made for pure driving pleasure. The 60° V-Motor accelerated the V-Rod smoothly from zero to 9,000 rpm and handled hills as if they were barely there. The unusually broad power band and the

A Harley-Davidson with a water pump? Still a horror to many traditionalists in the USA. The V-Rod is one of the most popular motorcycles in Europe.

Left: Disc wheel and design disc brakes.

Right: Typical V-Rod—the raked headlamp.

100Nm of torque produced by 1130 cc, left no doubt that a new era had begun. Porsche deserved a salute.

Once on top, it was time for the mandatory part of the program: photo shooting. After the motor was turned off an unusual sound filled the ears, a loud electric fan, which reduces the coolant temperature. The next stage was an intensive braking test: before entering the first curve I braked Harley fashion; consequently, I was going much too slow before I reached the curve. Everything that was known about this ignored component can now be consigned to the files. Even after covering approximately three miles (five kilometers) with tight curves and up to eleven percent grades, the braking power of the disc brakes was scarcely affected. The pressure point of the four-piston brake saddle can be felt, allowing the right amount of brake to be applied to stop the 594-pound (270-kilogram) bike. Previously, this

had only been possible on bikes from the Land of the Rising Sun. The familiar comfortable seating position, combined with familiar control elements, gave no reason to suspect that this cruiser also had sporting qualities.

Meanwhile, there have been additions to the V-Rod family. From the sport-oriented VRSCR model to the lower-priced VRSCB to the touring model and the first factory dragster anywhere, Harley-Davidson has developed a complete product palette from the bike, which will surely continue to grow.

Left: A touch of MV Augusta, but with much more chrome—Rod exhaust.

Right: Big twin riders are immediately at home. Control elements like all other Harleys.

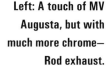

The superb and well laid-out instrument panel.

Below: The accessory catalogue delivered with the motorcycle— sissy bar and luggage rack.

Technical Data
VRSCA V-ROD (2001)

Frame:	Double loop steel tube frame, aluminum profile swing arm, 2 shock absorbers
Fork:	Telescopic fork
Motor:	Liquid-cooled V2, DOHC, fuel injection
Cylinders:	2, 60° cylinder angle
Displacement:	1131 ccm
Output:	120 hp
Construction Year:	2001-2007

FLSTS HERITAGE SPRINGER SOFTAIL (2003)
100 Years of Harley-Davidson

100 years of American iron: an orgy of paint, chrome and steel for Harley-Davidson's milestone birthday.

A deep bumble fills the air, as if a distant storm lay over Lake Michigan, but the rumble quickly grows louder, and like a harbinger, a police officer from Milwaukee comes down the road on a motorcycle, followed by another police escort. What followed was an hour-long parade of thousands and thousands of motorcycles in a roll-in show such as even Milwaukee had never seen. Harley-Davidson was celebrating 100 years in business—and the conclusion in Milwaukee was the high point of the year.

What was being celebrated was the first 100th birthday of a motorcycle company celebrated round the world. There were other celebrations in Japan,

Australia, Germany, and Spain—and everywhere, hundreds of thousands of Harley fans came to the events to celebrate the occasion in style.

For Harley-Davidson's design department, the milestone event had begun years earlier, with the development of colors, artwork, and posters of the birthday model for the 2003 model year. The manufacturer from Milwaukee celebrated its birthday with an unprecedented plethora of special paint finishes, birthday cards, and decals just for that model year. At least one machine from each series was offered in a special black and silver 100th Anniversary paint scheme, in

The jubilee rocker on the Twin Cam motor.

which the colors were divided by special decals with tiny "Harley-Davidson" wording separated by diamonds. As well there is the large tank badge with the "Bar and Shield" logo, wings and the number "100."

Thereby, even before its birthday, Harley indulged itself in a rejuvenation of its model range: with the introduction of the V-Rod in 2001 itself raising the bar for the birthday. The Power Cruiser was the most modern and revolutionary bike that had ever left the Harley assembly line—and a separate production facility was set up in Kansas to make it. Shortly before the company's 95th birthday, in Milwaukee Harley-Davidson, the course was set toward the future: The new Twin Cam 88 motor would be introduced in 1999, first on the FX and FL models with rubber-mounted motors. These would be followed the next year by the Twin Cam 88 B, the B standing for *balanced*. For the first time an air-cooled Harley twin would have balance shafts to compensate for vibration. All Softail models were equipped with the unit, which resulted in the Sportster series being stylized as "old timers" in the 2003 model year.

Inconspicuously but steadily, during its time in production, the Heritage Softail had assumed the position previously occupied by the Electra Glide: the light tourer with windshield, saddlebags, and running boards—the entire package in the popular Softail frame, which was reminiscent of the rigid frames of the Panhead and Knucklehead models. With a comfortable seat and spoked wheels, the Heritage Softail had exactly the retro look that Harley fans desired. Modern technology in old clothes, paired with a powerful motor from Milwaukee, still produced in that city for later marriage with the drive train in York, Pennsylvania. And then

The master switch also includes the ignition switch.

Left: Chrome power—so much comes together after 100 years.

Right: Springer fork nostalgia and modern disc brakes.

came the orgy of paint and chrome, which in birthday clothes of course promised special collector value. The anniversary model sold out quicker than any other Harley model year... The estimated 500,000 Harley fans who congregated in Milwaukee in the first weekend in September cared little about all that. They were celebrating what was probably the biggest birthday party the world had ever seen—and an entire major American city took part. For a weekend the city's brick buildings trembled from the thunder of the V-Twins, and the hotels and campgrounds for 125 miles (200 kilometers) around were booked up.

On that weekend, classic rock legends gathered in Henry W. Maier Festival Park on Lake Michigan, and stunt shows and motorcycle artists attracted more than Harley riders to the lake. The bikes were parked tightly in huge parking lots, creating a huge bike show. One only turns 100 once.

Every five years, clubs large and small from around the world come together for "Homecoming" and often ride across the USA to Milwaukee. There are celebrations all over the city—and the factory buildings where the motors are produced, especially the old factory on Juneau Avenue, are literally besieged by the visitors.

Left: Tombstone tail light.

Right: Modern times—the engine numbers are laser etched.

Where do jubilee badges belong? Tank (above), seat (center), and tank dash (below).

Technical Data

FLSTS HERITAGE SPRINGER SOFTAIL (2003) (100TH ANNIVERSARY)

Frame:	Double loop steel tube frame, Softail steel tube swing arm, 2 shock absorbers under the frame
Fork:	Telescopic fork
Motor:	Air-cooled V2 Twin Cam 88 B, OHV control, belt drive, 5-speed manual transmission
Cylinders:	2, 45° cylinder angle
Displacement:	88 cubic inches
Output:	approximately 64 hp
Construction Year:	2003

VRSCR STREET ROD (2006-2007)
It Only Danced Two Summers...

For true motorcycle riders the best machine Harley-Davidson ever put on two wheels: The Street Rod is pure riding pleasure.

With the introduction of the V-Rod in 2001, Harley-Davidson not only achieved a milestone for itself, it also approached the expectations of other models with liquid-cooled V-twins. Until the 2006 model year the conversion of the V-Rod into a "street burner" was left to dedicated dealers, and there weren't many of these, especially in the USA. In Europe the Harley dealer in Toulon built an experimental V-Rod with upside-down forks and variable handlebar geometry—but it remained a one-off. Harley-Davidson could also have taken that as a warning, for since 11 September 2001 the United States and France had been separated by more than the Atlantic. By that time, design work was too far advanced, and in the USA, sales of the V-Rod remained below expectations. Elsewhere V-Rod fans were delighted with the modern bike and its powerful 120 hp motor but had to put up with the foot pegs, which were placed too far forward on the frame and touched the ground in turns. Not until the Street Rod did Harley-Davidson make a quantum leap forward: Many considered the Street Rod the best Harley ever built. Despite its similarity to the VRSCA V-Rod, whose motor powers the machine, the Street Rod is a completely stand-alone motorcycle. High seat position, good ground clearance, mid-placed foot rest system and upside-down forks make the

Not until the Street Rod was the liquid-cooled Revolution motor really challenged.

Street Rod a true curve hugger. It is the first Harley since the XLCR Café Racer and the XR 1000 that can justifiably be called such. The technical solutions come from the V-Rod: injection system and air box under the false tank, with the real fuel reservoir beneath the seat, whose height can be adjusted from 25.9 to 30 inches (660 to 762 mm). The radiator is identical to that of the V-Rod and is difficult to replace even in conversion work: the flow of cooling air with eddies through the intake guide vanes is too complex. A replacement radiator would have to be almost twice as large to achieve the same effectiveness. The exhaust system was also raised to a point where it no longer causes sparks to fly in turns.

With a displacement of just 1131 cc, the machine would appear to be at a disadvantage compared to the 45° air-cooled motors. In day-to-day use, however, this is immediately compensated for. With 120 hp, throttle response is good and is sufficient to pull the machine, which has a dry weight of 649 pounds (295 kilograms), out of any corner. A precise-shifting five-speed transmission and low-maintenance belt drive transfer the power to the rear wheel. On country roads the Street Rod is a real revelation: one can race around corners without mercy, and the brakes and running gear are the very best. A 660-pound (300-kilogram) monster with handling like that of a super-moto artist – hard to believe that this machine comes from Milwaukee.

These doubts must also have come over potential buyers of the Street Rod,

The ignition switch is hidden in the steering head.

Left: Control
elements as usual,
hydraulic clutch.

Right: Design classic—
V-Rod headlight.

for both in the USA and in Europe
the bikes sat in the shops. Neither
enthusiastic reports in motorcycling
magazines nor finishing by custom
bike and street fighter specialists like
RRC and Speed Point could do anything
to change this. With engine tuning,
even more performance could be had
from the V-Rod—more than 150 hp
was possible. The true potential of the
Porsche-developed motor series was best
achieved with the new turbo kit from
Sprintex. These kits soon became hard
to find, but a Street Rod thus modified
put out 160 hp, capable of shooting the
bike from town to town. Owing to a lack
of demand, the Street Rod was removed
from the program in the 2008 model
year. Given the cost of development
associated with the design of the new
running gear and adequate accessories,
this was a not insignificant setback
for Harley-Davidson. The machine
that received the highest praise from
the experts was also the poorest seller.
Whether the V-Rod will experience a
resurrection depends on the future

development of the American market.
With the appearance of the new Buell it
seems rather unlikely. Anyone wanting
to combine the image of a Harley-
Davidson with the performance of a true
street bike can assure himself a true
future classic with the Street Rod—and
have fun on the road.

Left: The exhaust
system provides
excellent ground
clearance.

Right: The four-piston
calipers bite firmly
into the discs.

In one glance: speedometer, tachometer and fuel gauge.

Center: Integrated— tail light recessed in the fender.

Below: Aluminum accents wherever one looks.

Technical Data
VRSCR STREET ROD (2006-2007)

Frame:	Double loop steel tube frame, aluminum profile swing arm, 2 shock absorbers
Fork:	Upside-down
Motor:	Liquid-cooled V2, DOHC, fuel injection
Cylinders:	2, 60° cylinder angle
Displacement:	1131 ccm
Output:	120 hp
Construction Year:	2006-2007

XL 1200 N NIGHTSTER (2008)
...One For the Night

Harley-Davidson had never been lazy when it came to seeking out, testing, and filling gaps in the market: With the 2008 model year, the Sportster series grew to eight models—a tribute to the fifty-year history of the Sportster series, which was brought up to the technical standards of the new century with a rubber-mounted 1200 cc motor. Despite fifty years of continuous development, the 2008 Sportster has more in common with its ancestors than its name. Until very recently, the bike's running gear consisted of the 45° V-Twin with quad underhead cam system, direct-mounted transmission, displacement stages of 883, 1000 and 1200 cc (the "liter" has since been discarded) and twin-tube frame.

Despite its low displacement compared to the Big Twin models, the Sportster has always been the sportier Harley, and not just because of its name. The Harley-Davidson Sportster Cup is run with the fast twins—and almost every fast Harley-based V-Twin dragster has four camshafts. Based on experience with the FX models, the Sportster's entire motor housing is mounted on rubber blocks to almost completely prevent the vibration that Sportster riders have been enjoying for almost fifty years from reaching the frame. On account of stricter emission laws, the 2008 Sportster motor also has fuel injection. Harley calls it Electronic

A look with tradition: 2008 model year XL 1200 Nightster.

The 1200 Sportster motor: now finally seated in rubber mounts.

Sequential Fuel Injection, or ESPFI for short, and for those who do not enjoy tightening bolts themselves—which are most Harley-Davidson customers these days—are pleased about the system's low maintenance and reliability. The high-torque motor pulls the bike, whose weight has risen to 558.8 pounds (254 kilograms), smoothly through curves. Maximum lean clearance is 30° on the left and 29° right—1° is the cost of the cool-looking "slash-cut" exhaust system. To achieve a hotrod look, the bike has done away with the low seat, which had made it a first choice for shorter riders. Nevertheless, the Sporty is anything but a "lady's bike," something the Sportster models have often been called by the uninformed. After all, even Elvis Presley appeared with an earlier KH Model Sportster on the cover of the company magazine *Enthusiast*.

The Nightster is the latest model of the series for 2008 and visually it was trimmed to achieve a minimalist look. The old-style optics with spoked wheels and solo seat were based on Sportsters of the 1950s and 60s, but ultimately the old-timers look more compact and better designed. Perhaps this was just because

Ignition switch on the frame: The electrical components have multiplied in fifty years of Sportster history.

**Classic:
spoked wheels.**

**Right: Old school
look—bellows protect
the forks.**

**Right: Small but
effective—headlight.**

simply too many electrical components and cables had to be covered by too little metal? Or maybe one simply has to get used to the new look? Time will tell.

In exchange, Harley-Davidson again turned to innovative and extravagant design: For example, the backup and brake lights are no longer on the rear fender. Instead, they are located in the signal light housings.

Whether the new look will prove a success remains to be seen—the company did not take the risk of stepping into the new LED technology, however. In the USA, the license plate is even mounted on the side, a concession to the custom look often found in the most recent model years. Rims and hubs, forks and handlebars, even the foot rests and grips are black. Cover caps on the handlebars and holes in the belt cover underline the custom look. The motor and air filter are medium gray, making the Nightster a real looker—even during the day. And like all Harley-Davidsons, anything the

production bike fails to offer can be found in accessory catalogues, which today are almost part of a motorcycle's standard equipment. Anyone seeking a reasonably-priced and stylish entry-level bike will find the Nightster an ideal choice.

This bike is perfect for a cool ride along the beach promenade at St. Tropez, and then the country road to the north, and the curving roads of the Luberon or the French Alpine lakes. But wait until the sun comes up to enjoy it...

Left: Street legal—frying pan shaped rear-view mirrors.

Center: Minimalization—speedometer and control lamps.

Below: David Copperfield has struck—where is the tail light?

Technical Data
XL 1200 N NIGHTSTER (2008)

Frame:	Double loop steel tube frame, steel tube swing arm, 2 shock absorbers
Fork:	Telescopic fork
Motor:	Air-cooled V2 Evolution Sportster, OHV control, belt drive, 5-speed manual transmission, engine casing rubber-mounted, ESPFI fuel injection
Cylinders:	2, 45° cylinder angle
Displacement:	73.20 cubic inches
Output:	approximately 67 hp
Construction Year:	from 2008

FXD DYNA SUPER GLIDE (2008)
...And the Beat Goes On: 105 Years of Harley-Davidson

Which motorcycle was the oldest machine in the Harley-Davidson program in 2007? It is a question that challenges even the pros and experts on the Harley-Davidson scene and can earn you a beer too. The answer: the V-Rod! Who would have thought that Harley-Davidson, basking in the sun after its 100th anniversary, would be quickly disabused. The Street Rod, a completely new Sportster, and the increase in displacement to 96 cubic inches for the entire Big Twin line of 2008 stirred up the market and Harley's own dealers—especially since the increase in displacement was just a part of the new evolution. The running gear and hardware were also reworked as were

the electronics. In order to keep up with new exhaust emission standards in the most important world markets, Harley-Davidson had also equipped its entire line with fuel injection. This was not just to protect the environment—with the new diagnostic devices, customers were much more reliant on official dealers than before, because only they had the correct software for motors and machines. With this mixture, the Dyna Super Glide was one of the most modern motorcycles in the Harley lineup— thirty-seven years after its introduction! The models thirty-fifth production year had been celebrated in the 2006 model year—and the man responsible for

Elegant visuals: The birthday paint scheme for the company's 105th jubilee.

the design of the original Super Glide once again made the motorcycle the "Muscle Bike from Milwaukee." The thirty-fifth anniversary edition was in fact a high point of the series, with the same red-white-blue as the Stars and Stripes and the "1" logo on the tank. This time Willie G. didn't have to face a skeptical management; instead, he was able to draw from the full reservoir of a successful company history, much of which he had co-designed. Like the Corvette, the TransAm, or a Coca-Cola bottle, the Super Glide was unmistakably American. From its narrow front wheel to its fat tire in the back, from the "pull-back" handlebars to the wide, rounded rear metal fender which, supported by shiny chrome struts, covered the rear wheel—this motorcycle was a macho bike of the purest kind. In the years that followed, the Super Glide's paint work became rather less conspicuous. Not until the special 105th anniversary models did the full palette of colors return to some degree—the anniversary color combination was Anniversary Copper and Vivid Black. Regular celebrations were being held in Milwaukee every five years and 2008 was also the twenty-fifth anniversary of the founding of the Harley Owners Group, or HOG. Another reason to celebrate.

In many respects, the 2008 model year was a slice of company history, both because of the anniversary and the model changes. The new 96-cubic-inch motor was equivalent to earlier motors modified with Harley's own "Screamin Eagle" tuning kits. The factory figures were 78 hp at 5,000 rpm. This didn't put the tuners entirely out of business, but the 2008 motors had so much power and torque that no further performance increase seemed desirable. As on all FX models, the twin cam motor is mounted in rubber blocks, which shields the

rider from vibration. A silver powder coating also makes the V-Twin visually appealing. After the introduction of twin cam motors in 1999, the motor and transmission remained technically one unit, and for reasons of tradition the huge primary housing was retained. Inside the transmission housing, the rider has a choice of six gears, although the sixth gear is envisaged as an overdrive for comfortable cruising on

The most powerful Big Twin of all time: In previous years, 96 cubic inches could only be obtained as a tuning kit.

Copper insert in the Twin Cam side cover.

Into the next season with style: air filter over the injection system.

overdrive for comfortable cruising on the long American highways. In city traffic, or everyday European riding, the original five gears were completely adequate—the rest was taken care of by the generous torque. With the 5.1-gallon Fat Bob tank, the Super Glide now has undeniable touring qualities. The last attempt at a sport-tourer had used the transmission of the FXDXT Super Glide T-Sport, which had just a short production life.

Anyone who drives a Super Glide will be impressed, whether by the Custom Look, even fatter tires, non-stop performance or just a garish paint scheme. Anyone who purchases a motorcycle in the 105th anniversary paint scheme, however, gets free delivery: a collector's edition whose value is unlikely to fall. And one on which can be seen every five years in Milwaukee: Come celebrate!

Bottom: With new environmental laws, all Harley-Davidson models are now equipped with fuel injection.

Modern in technology, nostalgic in look: tank dash 2008.

Center: 105th anniversary badge on the tank leather...

Below: ...and on the tank.

Technical Data
FXD DYNA SUPER GLIDE (2008)
(105TH ANNIVERSARY EDITION)

Frame:	Double loop steel tube frame, steel tube swing arm, 2 shock absorbers under the frame
Fork:	Telescopic fork
Motor:	Air-cooled V2 Twin Cam 96, OHV control, belt drive, 6-speed manual transmission
Cylinders:	2, 45° cylinder angle
Displacement:	96 cubic inches
Output:	approximately 78 hp
Construction Year:	2008

VRSCDX NIGHT ROD (2008)
Street Fighter Deluxe!

A street fighter that is fun to drive: The Night Rod shines through inner value and a radical appearance.

If Harley-Davidson has learned anything from its 105 years of history, it is to carefully follow its customers' tastes and the spirit of the times. To this end, the company—especially since buying the firm back from AMF—has taken a series of measures, which has kept local dealers and the mother company in Milwaukee always close to the ear of present and future customers. On the one hand there is the Harley Owners Group (HOG), which invites Harley owners to a variety of special events, with owners arriving together or meeting there. The special colors, decorative in black and gold, create feeling of community and the dealers who look after the individual chapters can pick up on trends and wants and pass these up the

line. The second means—one extremely popular among fans and riders alike—is the ride-in bike show, which are held at the major motorcycle meets like Sturgis, Daytona, Faak, and most HOG rallies. "See and be seen" is part of the Harley feeling—as is showing off what one has.

The Wednesday of Bike Week in Daytona Beach, held the first week of March each year, belongs to the Harley-Davidson Ride-In Bikeshow, the proceeds of which traditionally go to the Muscular Dystrophy Association. Chrome-covered custom bikes, polished classics, and brightly painted full dressers roll past the Ocean Center

on Atlantic Avenue—with the Harley-Davidson indoor show the high point of activities for Harley fans. At the events held in the USA, experts from the technical and marketing departments take over the judging—and, in the process, see many ideas that in one way or another find their way into production. Willie G. Davidson also makes the rounds—as he does at other bike show classics like the Rat's Hole Show—and allows himself to be inspired. New ideas may not find their way into the next model year, but the company's memory is long.

Perhaps the best example of this is the VRSCD Night Rod. Of course, there is always the factor of ideas turning up in different places at the same time—and after five years, one can assume that this design, at some point, also lay on Harley-Davidson's table. The fact is, however, that in 2001, immediately after the V-Rod was introduced, a race to produce the first converted V-Rod began.

At the very front were Fred Kodlin and Speed-point Racing from Iserlohn. Even before Kodlin rolled out his F-Rod on the Saturday of Bike Week for its premier at the Rat's Hole Show, the Speed-point team brought two similarly modified V-Rods to the ride-in show in front of Ocean Center. They had a 240 rear tire, improved swing-arm, custom wheels, and a small handlebar fairing—one bike was white, the other overall black. Did they somehow look familiar? Willie G.

Left: Disc wheels, now with cutouts, matching the disc brake design.

Right: Belt drive to the rear wheel.

personally signed the bikes after the bike show, when Speed-point collected the trophy it had won. In fact, Harley-Davidson had already delivered an accessory catalogue with the V-Rod—yet an accessory maker had won the race to customize the V-Rod by a nose. The 2006 model line must have looked like déjà-vu to the Speed-point boys, even if the Night Rod differed from their custom bikes in several respects.

Not for nothing was the Night Rod shown on a drag strip at its unveiling. While the first model retained perforated disk wheels, in 2008, these were replaced by hot five-spoke wheels in the hotrod style. Welcome to the starting light. The black, powder-coated power plant gave the Night Rod a true race feeling.

In the 2008 model year, the Revolution motor was bored out to 1250 cc. The bore of each cylinder was increased from 3.9 to 4.1 inches (100 to 105 mm), while the stroke remained the same. The motor now produced 125 hp at 8,250 rpm, and anyone who wanted to race a Destroyer model at the drag strip could coax a few more horses. The new motor received a new clutch with twenty percent less lever force and—optionally—an ABS system, which improved safety considerably. Compared to the V-Rod, the Night Rod had a somewhat higher running gear—in fact, the Night Rod was supposed to close the gap between the V- and Street Rod. At least the exhaust system of the Street Rods delivered in 2007 was recyclable. With its cooler appearance, especially in Germany, the Night Rod shot to number one in the Harley registration statistics. A Night Rod Special was offered for the 2008 model year, with an even darker appearance and matte black exhaust system. A special 105th anniversary VRSCAW version was also released in 2008. The Night Rod's future still lies before it!

Bottom: Fittings and mirror from the Harley building block set.

Black and easy to see: the instrument console beneath the small fairing.

Center: Streamlined tail made of GFK.

Below: Recessed in the tail section— the tail light.

Technical Data **VRSCDX NIGHT ROD (2008)**

Frame:	Double loop steel tube frame, aluminum profile swing arm, 2 shock absorbers
Fork:	Telescopic fork
Motor:	Liquid-cooled V2, DOHC, fuel injection
Cylinders:	2, 60° cylinder angle
Displacement:	1250 cc
Output:	approximately 125 hp
Construction Year:	from 2008